PRAISE FOR *SACRED STRIDES*

"How can we give ourselves freely [...] the fullness of life in this world? [...] many other questions is one that J[...] and poetically in this book. McRob[...] ity of performance and the danger of overidentification with our work, and into the river of Belovedness that flows within everyone and everything. Justin shows us that we can create and enjoy. And I'm grateful that he does."

—KEVIN SWEENEY, AUTHOR OF *THE MAKING OF A MYSTIC* AND *THE JOY OF LETTING GO*

"Justin McRoberts takes a deep dive into what it means to live fully alive as the Beloved. I have benefited so much from his stories, guidance, and meditations. I highly recommend this book to anyone seeking a richer, more spirit-rooted experience of rest and meaningful work."

—STEPHEN ROACH, HOST OF *MAKERS & MYSTICS* PODCAST AND FOUNDER OF *THE BREATH & THE CLAY*

"Endorsements are weird. Do I speak of the book or its author? Yes. I've heard a wonderful quote about how one of the greatest gifts of the spiritual director is his living embodiment of the reality that the kind of life his pupil hopes is possible . . . actually is. Justin's life bears witness to the fruit of a practice that cultivates that kind of hope, distilled here in these Sacred Strides. If wisdom—in the words of David Bentley Hart—is 'the recovery of innocence at the far end of experience,' then I trust the wellspring these words came from. Justin's work (and rest) has helped me see it. *Sacred Strides* is an invitation to remember the Already that always is: Belovedness, at the center of everything."

—LEVI THE POET, SPOKEN WORD ARTIST AND AUTHOR

"With the sage offering of someone who's been there, done that, master storyteller Justin McRoberts offers readers a new and better way forward. *Sacred Strides* is a gift to those who live at the intersection of art and spirituality, who find a home in intersections of pastoring and creating. We need to laugh, just as we need to rest and be reminded of our divine Belovedness, and from the very first page, Justin extends an invitation that pushes holy buttons, in the very best way."

—CARA MEREDITH, AUTHOR OF *THE COLOR OF LIFE*

"We know our hustle culture is addictive and destructive, but what exactly does good work—and good rest—look like anyway? *Sacred Strides* is the answer for the worn-out, worked up, and weary follower of Jesus. With candor, humor, and warmth, Justin invites all of us to redefine our work and our rest, all the while rediscovering our Beloved status with God. Justin takes timeless truth and waves them in fresh air, giving us new hope for a different way to engage our pace and our purpose. I cannot wait to get this into the hands of pastors, leaders, and achievers of all kinds!"

—NICOLE UNICE, SPEAKER, AUTHOR OF *THE MIRACLE MOMENT* AND HOST OF *LET'S BE REAL* PODCAST

"What I have come to know to be true about Justin is clear in this book. He is hopeful, realistic, creative, and vulnerable in helping us find the meeting point between rest and work. This book is not only a needed and unique perspective in a well-worn discussion; it is hard-won, invaluable wisdom. Justin issues a clarion call to all of us—myself included—to rediscover our God, sanity, and our souls in both the way we cease and the way we strive. A book well worth your energy and reflection from someone for whom I am extremely grateful."

—CASEY TYGRETT, SPIRITUAL DIRECTOR AND AUTHOR OF *THE GIFT OF RESTLESSNESS*

"Generous, funny, compassionate, and wise, *Sacred Strides* inspired me to think about myself and my work in a new way. Justin takes us on an inspiring exploration of what it means to embrace our work and our calling without discarding ourselves. Highly recommended!"

—MATT MIKALATOS, AUTHOR OF *JOURNEY TO LOVE* AND *THE FIRST TIME WE SAW HIM*

"With honest, approachable storytelling, Justin undoes the narrative that work determines our worth. What a holy reminder that we don't have to perform our way into being called Beloved by God. In a weary world, *Sacred Strides* invites us to rest—and offers us a pen to write a new story about who we are."

—KAYLA CRAIG, AUTHOR OF *TO LIGHT THEIR WAY* AND COFOUNDER OF *UPSIDE DOWN* PODCAST

"Justin McRoberts writes books about faith that are for all of us, reflections that shine love and light on our paths no matter where we are on our spiritual journeys. With a grace and depth that's reminiscent of books by Henri Nouwen or Brennan Manning, *Sacred Strides* is a poetic and accessible expounding about becoming connected to God's ever-present rhythm. *Sacred Strides* is hopeful and earnest, a powerful call for each of us to discover, rediscover, and center our identities in the creative richness of God's love."

—MATTHEW PAUL TURNER, AUTHOR OF *I AM GOD'S DREAM* AND *OUR GREAT BIG AMERICAN GOD*

SACRED STRIDES

SACRED STRIDES

THE JOURNEY TO BELOVEDNESS
IN WORK AND REST

JUSTIN McROBERTS

W PUBLISHING GROUP

AN IMPRINT OF THOMAS NELSON

Sacred Strides

© 2023 Justin McRoberts

Published in Nashville, Tennessee, by W Publishing, an imprint of Thomas Nelson.

The author is represented by Alive Literary Agency, www.aliveliterary.com.

Thomas Nelson titles may be purchased in bulk for educational, business, fundraising, or sales promotional use. For information, please email SpecialMarkets@ThomasNelson.com.

Scripture quotations are from the Holy Bible, New International Version®, NIV®. Copyright © 1973, 1978, 1984, 2011 by Biblica, Inc.® Used by permission of Zondervan. All rights reserved worldwide. www.zondervan.com. The "NIV" and "New International Version" are trademarks registered in the United States Patent and Trademark Office by Biblica, Inc.®

Any internet addresses, phone numbers, or company or product information printed in this book are offered as a resource and are not intended in any way to be or to imply an endorsement by Thomas Nelson, nor does Thomas Nelson vouch for the existence, content, or services of these sites, phone numbers, companies, or products beyond the life of this book.

Some personal names and identifying details have been changed to protect the privacy of the individuals involved.

ISBN 978-0-7852-4000-6 (audiobook)
ISBN 978-0-7852-3981-9 (eBook)
ISBN 978-0-7852-3990-1 (softcover)

Library of Congress Control Number: 2022950303

Printed in the United States of America
23 24 25 26 27 LBC 5 4 3 2 1

For Asa and Katelyn

I hope and pray that you cherish and enjoy the life you've been given and that you know how perfectly and relentlessly you are loved while you live it.

CONTENTS

Contents

Prologue

WARMING UP (TO MY OWN BELOVEDNESS)

Just as the rhythm and tension between strides propel me forward when I run, I have found the rhythm and tension between work and rest (action and contemplation) awaken me to the Love of God and move me deeper into that Love.

I've collected the stories and reflections that make up this book to help you do meaningful work and rest deeply—and in both things to realize how deeply you are Loved by the God who just wants to be with you.

When I started running, I just wanted to be with my dad. My memory of him inviting me to run with him goes about as far back as I remember him. I mean, he wasn't taking me on ten-mile jogs when I was six years of age, but I remember running with my dad through Newhall Community Park in Concord, California, when I was twelve. He'd be a step or two in front of me and calling over his shoulder, "Pick up the pace a little" or "Just try to keep up."

All I wanted to do was be with him while he ran. I wasn't all that interested in getting into shape or winning races. I liked running with my dad because he was my dad. My neighbor Jason went duck hunting with his dad. Chris went surfing with his dad. Braden worked with his dad on weekends, framing houses and putting up drywall.

My dad loved running. He came home energized, happy, and even looking a bit younger. I suppose I felt very much the same when he invited me to run with him; energized, happy, and young. That's pretty near the heart of Belovedness—simply being with the one you love. God wants you and me doing work that lights our hearts on fire. More than that, God wants to be with us in that work. God also wants you and me resting deeply from that (or any other) work—and he wants you and me to rest in and with him when we do. I don't think God is hoping we become more efficient and effective workers or even well-rested children. I think God simply wants to be with us.

So I don't want to just learn how to *work* well and wisely. Nor do I simply want to learn how to *rest*. What I want is to *live a full life with God* both in work and in rest. I want the same for you.

Running together remained a key connection point between my dad and me until I lost him to depression and suicide in 1998. To this day, I still remember our last run. It was really hard. It was hard for him physically and hard for both of us emotionally. We barely got in two of the four and a half miles we'd planned to run before he started falling apart. His left knee hurt from a fall he had taken a few months previously, and he couldn't maintain his rhythm or pace.

He limped a bit as we headed back to the car, and I remember him trying to hide his face so I couldn't see that he was crying. "I'm sorry I can't keep up," he said.

I was in my midtwenties at the time and in decent running shape. But I didn't need him to "keep up." I just wanted him to be with me because I loved him. I know now how hard my dad struggled to believe the simple truth that he was just plain loved.

So I moved around to his weak side, lightly grabbed his wrist, and threw his arm over my shoulders. We finished the last half mile that way, arms around each other and walking step-by-step together. His weakness meant room for a strength in me, which meant connection—and that's all I ever really wanted.

Maybe you're like me and devotion or rest or prayer doesn't come naturally. Like my dad's bad knee, that's my "weak side." I hope that, as you read, you sense the Spirit of God come alongside you and say, *I've got you. Just stay with me. That's all I want.*

Or maybe you've struggled to find and do meaningful work up to this point. Again, I hope you feel the Spirit of God come alongside you and say, *I've got you. Just stay with me. That's all I want.*

Chapter 1

GETTING OFF ON THE RIGHT FOOT

or

IT ALL COMES DOWN TO BEING LOVED

Having lived and worked in the arts and in professional ministry since 1998, I've felt the tension between hustle and self-care thicken and become wildly problematic. First, this conversation-turned-argument seems to suggest that one is more important than the other—that one season of life necessitates an emphasis on work, while another season calls and allows for rest; in the end one is more vital and more pleasing to God.

Second, the tension between work and rest is problematic because it suggests they are naturally opposites and in competition with each other.

On both counts, I disagree entirely.

In cultures focused on the spiritual disciplines, conversations about work and rest are often framed in terms like *contemplation* and *action*. For instance, Thomas Merton wrote, "Contemplation is the loving sense of this life, this presence and this eternity. . . . Action is the stream, and contemplation is the spring."[1] Many years later, Parker Palmer picked up this same thread. In *The Active Life*, Palmer observed that there is no competition between contemplation and action and that the apparent division between work and rest is a matter of practiced misunderstanding. He wrote, "Contemplation and action are integrated at the root, and their root is in our ceaseless drive to be fully alive."[2]

Getting Off on the Right Foot

Personally, I've boiled it down to this short poem:

> My natural posture is not work
> Nor is my natural posture rest
> My natural posture is Belovedness.
> Both work
> and rest
> spring from my Belovedness,
> and return me to it.

At no point in these pages will you find me prescribing some kind of balance between work and rest. I don't think that's how life works or how God designed you to live. Instead, I'll point to and celebrate the natural tension and rhythm between work and rest that I've experienced and grown from.

> At no point in these pages will you find me prescribing some kind of balance between work and rest. I don't think that's how life works or how God designed you to live.

This is a bit like saying it isn't *balance* between the left and right sides of my body that propels me forward on a journey; it is tension and rhythm. I stride forward with my left leg, planting my left foot and trusting the weight of my whole self to that side . . . and then in the next movement I stride forward with my right leg, planting my right foot and trusting the weight of my whole self to that side. It's not my left side that moves me more than my right; it is the tension and rhythm between them that moves my whole self.

This is a book about discovering and learning to practice a wholeness that cannot be achieved only by action and cannot be established only through contemplation. It is a gift offered in patient grace that is practiced in both work and rest. I can't hand it to you; that's for God to do. But I can tell you what it looked like for me when I stretched out my hand to Jesus as the leper did when he was made whole (Matthew 12:13).

The way I've come to share this journey with clients who've hired me as a coach and people I get to work with on retreats I lead is by telling stories like the ones I'll share throughout this book. I've discovered and come to believe deep truths about myself as a laborer for and with Christ, guided by the Spirit, and as a worshiper of God the Father. I am not, in essence, a useful tool in God's tool belt, predominately valued for my gifts and talents. I am also not an ascetic monk seeking to abandon daily life in order to find God somewhere in the desert (metaphorically or geographically) outside the noise and busyness of a productive life. I am Beloved by the One Who Holds All Things Together, including my need to work and my need to rest.

Without question, the most substantial learning curve on my journey toward Belovedness has been the practice of rest and Sabbath keeping. I naturally prefer working. I gravitate toward action and making things. For that reason, I consider rest the most *vital* aspect of my journey up to this point, in large part because rest has helped me to know I am Beloved in and through my work and not as a reward for it!

For years, I believed wholeness and spiritual fulfillment were available to me only if I could ignore or even reject my love of

> I am Beloved in and through my work and not as a reward for it!

work. Instead, the practice of rest has sanctified and clarified my work life, in much the same way as happens in music. In music, the rests between notes give shape, structure, and texture to a song. Those notes and the rests between them aren't opposites. Far from it. They are both essential elements of a song.

Before you go any further, I'd feel a bit better if I clarified a few terms I'll use more heavily in the following pages. One way to think about this list might be to consider these terms as a cast of characters who will appear throughout the story. Fyodor Dostoevsky's books often feature a very helpful character list—in part because there are so many to keep track of and in part because some of those characters have names like Agrafena "Grushenka" Alexandrovna Svetlov, who is not directly connected to Pavel Fyodorovich Smerdyakov, even though they both show up in parts of the same story adjacent to Ippolit Kirillovich.

My list is somewhat predictable. In this book, I'll use the words *rest, Sabbath, utility, work* versus *job,* and *Belovedness* quite a bit. So here's what's usually going on in my head when I do.

REST

When I use the word *rest,* I certainly do mean time away from my job and my work. But I don't think of rest as simply the absence of work. I also don't think rest is the *opposite* of work. I think a deeper dive into my earlier allusion to music theory might be helpful here. I promise not to make this long or academic because, to be entirely honest, even as a songwriter myself, I can handle only a little bit of music theory.

In music theory, a *rest* is the period of time a player is not playing a note on their instrument. But far from being just an absence, the rest between active notes holds integral space for the song as a whole. That space is every bit as important to the song as the notes or chords surrounding it. In fact, without rests, a song becomes muddy, messy, and chaotic. I'll even go so far as to say that often the structure of a song is held together by the space between notes. So while you certainly don't have a song if you don't have any notes, those spaces of rest between notes give the song shape it wouldn't have without them.

SABBATH

As a simple, strict definition of *Sabbath*, I lean pretty heavily on Mark Buchanan's description from his book *The Rest of God: Restoring Your Soul By Restoring Sabbath*. In it, he suggests the Sabbath is a full day of rest from work, every week, committed to God.[3]

Key for me is that, when I talk about Sabbath, I *do* mean a whole day. I get that taking a half day or cutting work off early can feel sabbath-y or sabbath-like, but those references need an origin. And the origin of that sabbath-y feeling you might get while driving away from your job at two fifteen instead of five thirty is that you and I are designed and commanded by God to set aside a full day on our calendar every week.

I also notice the way hyperreligious people in Scripture regularly had problems with the way Jesus behaved on the Sabbath. And I don't think the heart of the matter was poked at with questions like "Can I work on the Sabbath?" Instead, I think the way Jesus disappointed people's cultural expectations of Sabbath behavior drew out a better question:

"What works for you?"

When I talk about Sabbath, I hold in mind the striking moment in which a group of Pharisees jumped all over Jesus' disciples for picking heads of grain to eat because it was a Sabbath day. Jesus didn't get into a long debate with them about the texts they might have been referring to or the interpretation of those texts. Instead, he told a story about someone else bending the rules because of their circumstances and then said, "The Sabbath was made for man, not man for the Sabbath" (Mark 2:27).

Far from questioning whether or not it was a commandment or whether or not it was important, Jesus made it abundantly clear that the Sabbath commandment is important because of what it means for God's Beloved Ones.

Just like "Don't kill one another" and "Don't steal one another's stuff" are commandments about ensuring you and I get to live more fully and freely, so it is with keeping the Sabbath. It's not about getting it right; it's about living fully in the Love and goodness of God.

Which leads me back to the question "What works for you?" I think *how* you Sabbath is a conversation you get to have in kindness and care with people who know you and help you know yourself. It's a question that has a lot to do with how you live and who you are and what your preferences are as well as your needs.

UTILITY

The danger of utility as a guiding and dominant principle for life is that it puts me in the service of whatever power sets the agenda and the terms for success or value. If that power isn't the will and desire of the God who made me to be fully loved, I'll end up somewhere I don't want to go—namely, anywhere other than firmly in the arms of God.

Now, I really like being helpful. In fact, learning to be helpful has been a significant part of my spiritual maturity. Being self-expressive or even self-absorbed has been a bit of a natural pitfall for me. The time I've spent around servant-minded people has refined my posture, both professionally and personally. After years of working and living with people who take sincere joy in offering the best of who they are to the plans and dreams of others, I now take *much* deeper joy in knowing I can offer strengths and talents in the service of God's work than I ever did while trying to make a name for myself.

But while being useful can be a beautiful characteristic in a healthy relationship, personal or institutional, being *only* or even *primarily* useful can erode and distract one's soul. Much like the experience and expense of fast food becomes a tasty distraction from healthy eating, it can feel really, really good to be useful.

For a while.

But "useful" is not what I was created to be.

WORK VERSUS JOB

Because developing a healthier understanding of my work life plays a significant role in the following pages, I want to be as clear as I can about the words *work* and *job* and their relationship.

My *work* is the active, embodied expression of my love in and for the world around me. More deeply than that, my work is the shape divine Love takes in and through my life.

A *job* is something I do that pays for food and housing and clothing so that I can do my work.

My friend and mentor Frank has had a lot of jobs. He owned the record label I was on in the late '90s. He also owned a pizza place that had a mini golf course and a Starbucks kiosk inside it. He liked his jobs, but not because he felt a calling about music or pizza; he'd tell you he did those things to help other people's dreams happen, because that's the heartbeat of his life's work. His best and deepest work is being a great dad and helping his kids attain their dreams.

My friend Mike is a pastor. That's his job, and he's good at it. But he'd tell you the real work of his life is helping other pastors live more deeply in their Belovedness.

I know people whose jobs are in grocery stores or cubicles, but their work is being great neighbors to the folks who live across the street from them, as well as to the folks who live *on* the streets or under a nearby bridge.

When one's job is closely aligned to one's work, that can be very satisfying. But sometimes, depending on the nature of the work someone is called or compelled to do, a job is best when it supports that work. On the other hand, when a job is out of alignment with a work calling in someone's soul, it can be problematic when that job doesn't facilitate the execution of that person's work calling, either because of the amount of time the job takes or because the job takes all of their energy and focus or joy.

Right now, my job is to write this book. Doing this job contributes to my work. So, what is my work? My work is to provide helpful, clarifying language for your process and practice of life. I've done that work in a lot of ways during the past couple of decades. Which is to say, I've had a number of different jobs that have allowed me to do my work. I've had the jobs of Young Life leader, songwriter, producer, pastor, song leader, podcaster, coach, and so on.

Today, my job title is "author." I hope that this job sets me up to give the best of my work to you and that you find language in the following pages that is helpful and clarifying for your process and practice of life.

Speaking of language, I've got one more word for you.

BELOVEDNESS

It's possible that in every book I've written up to this point, I've made some reference to Jesus' baptism. I suppose I'm just not over that moment, and I hope I never am. I don't want you to be either.

In Matthew 3:17, God said:

This is my Son, whom I love; with him I am well pleased.

That moment and those words do more than touch something in me. They cut through other things to uncover and expose what is most real in and about me:

Belovedness is not just the most fundamental truth of Jesus' life; it is the most fundamental truth of yours and mine as well.

You're mine. I love you. I'm proud of you.

It's fair to say that those words and that moment are why I wrote this book. I want you to hear, *You're mine. I love you. I'm proud of you*—and know it's *you* God is talking to.

Belovedness is not just the most fundamental truth of Jesus' life; it is the most fundamental truth of yours and mine as well. It is also one of the most (if not *the* most) confoundingly and tragically elusive realities in human experience. In part because it is the thing every dark force in history most violently and vehemently seeks to distract you from and keep you from knowing. Because when you see yourself as Beloved, everything changes. This reality undoes every ruthless and inhumane system ever to enslave and diminish a human life.

There is nothing more vital, nothing more powerful, and nothing more true. In fact, on the other side or underside of Belovedness there is nothing at all. Belovedness is the intended and destined end of all things, just as it was their blessed and joyful beginning.

> When you see yourself as Beloved, everything changes.

Questions for Reflection

- Which of the above definitions stood out to you? Why do you think that is?
- Do you tend to feel better when you're working, or do you feel more whole when at rest?
- How do you respond to the word *Beloved*? Does that sound right? Is it awkward?

Chapter 2

A FALSE START

or

TAKE-YOUR-KID-
TO-WORK DAY

I have a lot of great memories about my dad getting ready for work in the mornings. Every morning, he'd put on the suit and tie he had set out the night before and leave with a clean-shaven face. He wore Old Spice and had a whole routine about putting it on before he'd throw on his white button-up shirt. Even as a twelve- or thirteen-year-old boy, I remember being inspired by my dad's professionalism and marveling at his work ethic. I knew he worked hard, and I liked that. I wanted to be that way. He seemed to like it too. But what I learned over time is that a lot of the energy my dad had for his work came from fear and anxiousness. Looking back now, I can see it as an overall pattern, but even in my youth there were moments when his fear and worry showed itself clearly.

I remember my dad inviting me to help him set up an office for a new business venture. After more than twenty-five years of working on other people's projects on other people's time, he had taken the risk of developing an idea of his own and was putting it together, largely from scratch. I remember sitting on the floor surrounded by stacks of envelopes and letters and books of stamps. The office didn't have furniture yet.

The business, called M&H Travel, was a consolidation point for travel agencies all over the San Francisco Bay Area. Working primarily with Air France, my dad was doing something like KAYAK and Priceline do now, well before the internet; he was saving hours of time for folks who were looking for the best travel deals by putting the information in one place. It was a really good idea, and there weren't many people attempting anything like it at the time.

After folding what had to be a few hundred letters and stuffing the envelopes, I was licking stamps and quickly pressing them onto the upper corners of those same envelopes. I don't remember exactly how many I'd gotten to, but it was enough that, by the time my dad noticed how sloppy I had been, I was in a fair amount of trouble.

"What are you doing?"

I thought very briefly about responding with a joke. But the look on my dad's face stopped that idea dead in its tracks. He was horrified.

Snatching up a handful of envelopes from the floor in front of me, he knelt down and began peeling off as many stamps as he could, replacing them more squarely.

"Dammit! Dammit! . . . They can't be this sloppy!"

I have often imagined how this moment might have gone. In my fantasy, my dad sits down on the floor with me to talk about professionalism and care. He teaches me about making people feel thought of and considered, convincing me that slowing down and taking the extra time to make things look and feel better communicates respect and (given the right context) even love.

That's not how it happened, though.

I picked up a few of the sloppy envelopes and started to help. But within moments of my doing so, he had swept my entire pile into his, mumbling, "Just give those to me. I'll do it."

He wasn't mad. Not really. He was scared. While I didn't recognize what was happening at the time, I know now that my dad was terrified of what would happen if his business failed. That fear not only stole a moment he and I might have shared (a moment a bit more like my wishful scenario above), but eventually that fear would steal from him the joy of work and even life itself.

After growing up in a household wracked by poverty, my dad entered an industry in which he was taught and trained that a man's worth was almost entirely about how useful he was. My dad wasn't taught that his strengths and talents were gifts given him by a God who'd made him that way in Love. To him, they were just tools intended to help him achieve specific ends—namely, fending off poverty and providing financially for those for whom he was responsible. In fact, I think it's no exaggeration at all to suggest that my dad was taught he was an instrument to be used by the companies he worked for, an instrument that could make my life better not by his simple presence but by the things he could provide.

So as he snatched those envelopes out of my hands, my dad, I think, was actually afraid that if he failed, he would prove himself less useful to his employer and to my mom and to me. And if he was less useful, he thought he wouldn't be as worthy

> I think the question just beneath the surface of "What must I do to be successful?" or "What must I do to become famous?" or even "What must I do in order to be fit and attractive?" is always "What must I do to be loved?"

of love and certainly not as able to care and provide for the people he wanted to care and provide for.

I think the question just beneath the surface of "What must I do to be successful?" or "What must I do to become famous?" or even "What must I do to be fit and attractive?" is always "What must I do to be loved?" And to me, the question feels a lot like the question that young man asked Jesus when he said, "What good thing must I do to get eternal life?" (Matthew 19:16).

"Why do you ask me about what is good?" Jesus replied. "There is only One who is good. If you want to enter life, keep the commandments."

"Which ones?" he inquired.

Jesus replied, "'You shall not murder, you shall not commit adultery, you shall not steal, you shall not give false testimony, honor your father and mother,' and 'love your neighbor as yourself.'"

"All these I have kept," the young man said. "What do I still lack?"

Jesus answered, "If you want to be perfect, go, sell your possessions and give to the poor, and you will have treasure in heaven. Then come, follow me." (vv. 17–21)

What I hear Jesus saying here is something like "You're asking about 'eternal life.' That's something I want to give you. You seem to want to earn it. But the kind of love you can earn isn't going to last. So ditch all that and come follow me; I'll get you where you really want to go."

I think the real problem with hustle and productivity culture in general isn't an overemphasis on work or even the push to put a lot of hours into one's work. Where I think hustle and productivity go wrong is the subtle (and sometimes not-so-subtle) promise that if you're useful and effective enough, it earns you the right to be loved, that Belovedness can be established in and through usefulness.

When my dad left his impoverished and abusive home just after high school, I think he went in search of places and ways to experience the Belovedness his upbringing lacked. What he was promised by the industry culture(s) that greeted him conveyed this message: "Jon, if you do these things and do them well, you will have loved your family. In return, you will become lovable and be loved yourself."

Of course, that message rarely gets communicated so clearly and directly, but if you listen carefully enough, you can hear whispers that sound less like the loving invitation of Jesus and a lot more like "If you do these things well, you will be loved by friends and family and fans and colleagues."

A False Start

I don't want anything to do with that invitation. I don't want you to accept it either.

Earlier this year, I took my now twelve-year-old son, Asa, to work with me. I'd been working on a few new songs and booked a studio session at a time I knew he could join me. He wasn't just coming to watch, which he'd done before. This time I'd asked him to play piano and sing with me. Over the previous few months, Asa and I had tinkered around with a pair of songs. I really liked the way they felt and sounded. He and I also wrote a few melodies for those songs, and I kept hinting that I was going to record those parts with him. For the most part, he thought I was joking.

I wasn't.

Not in the least.

I picked him up from school and drove toward the studio while listening to a recording we'd made at home. He was squirmy and jittery and was wearing the biggest smile. He's got one of those smiles that makes you want to smile too. When we finally parked, he paused for a moment before getting out of the car. "I just hope I don't mess it up." My heart leapt backward about twenty-nine years to me sitting on the floor of my dad's office realizing I'd messed up pretty bad with those stamps and being afraid of what that might mean. So I knew a little bit about the fear Asa was talking about. I also knew what I wished that moment had been like for me twenty-nine years earlier. And while I'll never get to replace that memory with my wishful version of it, there I was outside the studio where I do the work I care about, being given a chance to make a better memory with my Beloved son.

"Asa, there's no way you're going to mess this up. Actually, this is already perfect. I mean it. You're a good piano player, and you know I like your note choices. But the real deal for me here is that I like playing music with you. I just want you doing this with me. That's it."

He smiled and grabbed my hand.

I did my best not to embarrass him by crying like Matthew McConaughey's character in the movie *Interstellar*. But I'm bad at that, so I cried a little bit and he got a little embarrassed.

"We're going to have some fun today and make a song we wrote come to life," I assured him. "That's all I want. You into that?"

Is Asa the best piano player available to me? Not at all. But truth be told, I'm not the best guitar player available to me either. Yet I play guitar on all my own records because when I'm recording the songs I've written, it's not primarily about making things sounds good. Sure, that's part of it. But recording my music is about expressing who I am as a Beloved child of God. Each song and album is, at its heart, a work of love. The One Who Loves Me gave me these gifts and has guided me through the seasons that birthed these stories and melodies.

Asa is part of that now.

He's my son.

A False Start

My Beloved son.

He's mine. I love him. I'm proud of him.

Once we were in the studio, Asa took a few moments to listen to the track, took a deep breath, and then cut loose on the piano, playing the notes he heard in his head. Over the next few hours, he played and sang with joy and confidence. And he did so because his efforts were flowing from the knowledge that he was wanted there; he knew he was Beloved.

I think that's the heart of truly good work. Far from being a way to prove I am worthy of love, good work flows from Belovedness.

The story my dad believed growing up was that work automatically comes with stress or worry and that it is pretty much always about the bottom line. He was also convinced that experiencing any kind of love or joy along the way was a neat bonus but not essential or important.

That's not true. None of it.

And part of how I know none of that trash is true is because I know what it cost for my dad to believe it. It cost me my dad, it cost my kids their grandfather, and it cost my mom her husband.

Beloved, far from being a way to prove your worthiness, work is a way you and I get to love our world and the people in it. Regardless of your specific job, it is the love you experience and pass on that matters. So when your particular job ends or the work focus shifts or your abilities evolve and change, you still get to go on loving people with your time and talent. And it will be that love that matters. Any system or plan or structure that tells you otherwise is either blindly wrong or just plain lying.

> Regardless of your specific job, it is the love you experience and pass on that matters.

A few years into my dad's time with M&H Travel, Air France restructured its operations in a way that forced the closure of his office. He was devastated. I remember him being despondent and distant for a long time. He wouldn't tell me what was going on when I asked him, and I later learned he didn't talk to my mom much about it either.

I moved home to be around him because I was worried. My mom was worried too. He had some good days here and there, but my dad never actually came around. Instead, at fifty-five, he felt that the most useful thing he could do was to end his own life and leave my mom and me with the insurance money.

I'd trade every dime of what he left us to have him in my life.

The day of my father's memorial service, I heard women and men he'd worked with tell stories about the ways he'd made life better and richer for them, professionally and personally. Stories about his humor and kindness were sandwiched between stories of his intuition and commonsense wisdom. I was so proud to be the son of the man those stories were about.

A False Start

They were stories about him loving and caring for people. That was the legacy he left and the effect he had all along.

But my dad didn't see it. I don't want that to be the case for you. He'd been taught and trained to believe work wasn't about love at all. To him, work was just the thing he had to do because there were bills to pay. Work was a matter of strict utility. The most valuable thing he believed he could be in a system like that was *useful*.

> You are invited to love the world around you and the people in it. Not because you're useful. You're invited because you're Beloved.

That's not true. And believing it is true can cost you everything that matters. I don't want that for you. I really don't.

In and through the work you do, even today, regardless of your job, you are invited to love the world around you and the people in it. Not because you're useful. You're invited because you're Beloved.

Questions for Reflection

- Did your mom or dad have a job you were interested in when you were growing up? What was it?
- What or who did you want to be when you grew up? Why? Do you still dream about it?
- What do you *love* to do now? What makes you feel alive?

Chapter 3

STAYING IN MY LANE

or

GETTING FIRED AND
LEARNING TO CARE

'Ve been fired. Twice.

Both times, it was from jobs that required me to supervise children.

I know. Yikes.

In the case of my second sacking, I was substitute teaching at a private school down the road from my house. I had broken up a fight between a pair of kids in the class. Actually, calling it a "fight" is a bit misleading. It was just one bigger kid beating the fourth-grade snot out of a smaller kid. I got between them, separated them with my outstretched arms, and then told the bigger kid to "back the hell up."

That kid backed up all the way to the principal's office, where he told her I'd been cursing in class. I sat in her office for a solid fifteen minutes hearing about the impact of foul language on children's precious souls while concurrently learning (for the first time in my life, I might add) that *hell* was considered a bad word. I didn't notice much conversation in that meeting about the actual impact of fists on the other kid's precious face, and while I didn't point that out, I did point out that Jesus used the word *hell* in the Bible lesson we'd referenced earlier in the day. I'm pretty sure that's the point at which I was fired. I'm also

29

pretty sure the bigger kid winked at me on my way out the door once the meeting was over.

The other time, I'd been hired as a summer day care supervisor, and I wasn't supervising with much attention to detail. For example, at one point a kid in my group climbed up the back of the baseball backstop, fell off, and had the air knocked out of him. He limped into the office of the director to tell him he was hurt.

I didn't see any of it happen.

I wasn't paying attention.

I was really bad at that job.

Now Dennis, the gentleman who had hired me for this position, had done so because he'd seen me do improv. That's right, he saw me in a comedy sketch and thought, *The guy with the jokes should work with children!*

My friends and I had started a comedy sketch night for the city of Concord and, because he was an employee of the city, Dennis had been to one of our shows. One of the sketches we did that night was called "Hunter and Prey." The sketch was pretty much me making my way to the center of the stage, where I ended up wrestling a stuffed bear and losing. It was entirely silly but got a lot of laughs. To add to the silliness of the sketch, I would often approach the stage from the audience, climbing between and over and under the folding metal chairs on the floor.

Because it was a relatively full house on the night my future employer was present, I approached the stage from the floor, making a bit of a commotion as I did. One audience member didn't appreciate that part of the sketch, and, as I slinked between his feet, he grabbed me by the back of my thrift-shop-issue camouflage jacket, lifted me from the floor to be eye to eye, and said, "I'm trying to watch the show!"

"Sir," I said. "I *am* the show."

Something about that moment must have struck Dennis as genius because, just a few weeks later, I was on a dusty baseball diamond while one of the kids I was there to supervise locked himself in the janitor's hall closet until he was discovered by the janitor nearly an hour and a half later. I had no idea he was missing. In fact, I only learned about the whole episode when Dennis came to ask me what had happened to Zach.

That's one of the tricky things about being identified as "talented." Too often, being talented can become a mask for all kinds of substantial deficiencies, including a lack of wisdom and care.

"Which one is Zach?" I said.

Obviously, I wasn't the right person for that job. But Dennis had found me so entertaining, I think he figured my penchant for humor would somehow translate into being a good day care worker. That's one of the tricky things about being identified as "talented." Too often, being talented can become a mask for

31

all kinds of substantial deficiencies, including a lack of wisdom and care. That was doubly true for me as I identified *myself* as "talented." I learned to expect those capacities to cover faults in my character and my work. I liked kids, and I could make them laugh. But boy oh boy I wasn't ready to be responsible for the well-being and safety of someone else's child.

On the fateful day I actually got the axe, it was close to one hundred degrees outside, and I had been asked to come up with some kind of outdoor activity for nine kids. It had been pretty warm before, and outdoor activities had included things like sitting in the shade, lying down in the shade, and not going outside but telling Dennis we did. Other times, when it wasn't quite as hot, we went out to play games like freeze tag, hide-and-seek tag, play-dead tag, and regular tag.

That afternoon, I decided to change things up. In part because all nine kids were looking at me like *Don't you dare say "tag."* So I stood in the field adjacent to the day care center and said, "It's really hot today, guys."

They all nodded.

"Like, it's so hot I don't think I want to play tag."

Pretty much every head nodded in agreement.

"Let's take a drive."

Their excitement at the idea was all the confirmation I needed that I'd struck day care gold with this creative solution. Of course, even the best of ideas comes along with a short list of obstacles. Mine included:

1. I drove a 1992 Honda Civic Hatchback.

2. That car only had seat belts for five people, including me, the driver.

3. There were nine kids in my group.

You may notice that words like *illegal* or *irresponsible* didn't make an appearance on my list. Yeah, I noticed that too.

Now, before I get to the details of what happened next, I'll admit that this was nowhere near the first or the last time I tried to cram that car with things that didn't fit. I once tried to bring home a full-sized couch from the side of the road. And then there was the time I tried to get a Jet Ski into that car. Whoever brought the Jet Ski to the lake that day didn't have a plan for getting it back, and while I don't remember many of the details surrounding their faulty planning, I definitely recall saying something like "No big deal. I've got it. I drive a 1992 Honda Civic Hatchback. I can make it work."

Maybe that sounds ridiculous to you, but the way it played out in my mind was that people ride *on* Jet Skis but they ride *in* 1992 Honda Civic Hatchbacks. Smaller things should fit into the bigger things, right? So that had to mean Jet Skis would fit in a 1992 Honda Civic Hatchback.

Staying in My Lane

Two hours and two hundred feet of rope later, I was apparently wrong.

I wasn't wrong about getting nine kids into that car, though. That was easy. I put all the seats down, and they gleefully crawled in like feral cats. Once inside, they immediately started chanting, "Air-con-di-tion-ing!" (clap, clap, clap-clap-clap). So I fired up the AC, and we drove in loops around the parking lot for thirty minutes, listening to Run-DMC (the only tape I had in my car at the time).

I was fired the next morning. Turns out, the air-conditioned adventure I'd taken the kids on was a highlight for a few of them who just couldn't *wait* to tell their parents about it.

Maybe you're like me in that I don't enjoy learning my limits. I never have. Instead, I've tended to hope my creativity, ingenuity, and hard work would be like magic wands for pretty much any problem. I felt like I could create or outsmart or outwork my obstacles and limitations. But being fired from a job supervising kids was really embarrassing. It meant I was wrong about the magic quality of my gifts and talents. Not only because they were insufficient for overcoming any and every limitation but, more importantly, because I'd just learned that my gifts and talents were a sad replacement for actually caring about people.

Over time, care would have to become the context in which my strengths and abilities found their place. Either that or I'd end up hurting people. I almost did that day, which is a thing I didn't even think about until Dennis pointed it out while letting me go.

"You were one turn away from driving onto the street. Anything could have happened at that point." He was right. I was one turn away from a story that wouldn't have been funny at all. And that's what mattered to the parents who called Dennis about my employment. They didn't care how entertaining I was.

Not. At. All.

The entire purpose of the job I was hired to do was the *care* of those kids. It didn't matter one bit if I was funny or creative or clever. Those characteristics *might* have been bonus features. But what those parents primarily wanted when they signed their kids up for summer day care wasn't that their kids were entertained. They simply wanted to know that their Beloved children were safe and happy. That was the job, and they didn't think I was capable of (or interested in) doing that job.

And they were right.

I wasn't.

I was enchanted by the idea that my talents and creativity were the tools for every job, and the *only* way I learned they weren't was that I applied those gifts and talents and failed. And not just at the job as it was on paper. I had failed to care for people.

That was a tough thing to realize about myself—that I didn't actually care. And all these years later, it gives me shivers to write it. Learning that about myself in such a way pressed the knowledge into my psychology the way a needle presses a tattoo into skin. If this were an actual tattoo in my mind, it would be of a 1992 Honda Civic Hatchback with a Jet Ski falling out the back of it, and it would read "My talents don't matter if I don't care."

Care sets the stage for all of our strengths and talents. The real question is pretty much *never* about how gifted and capable you are. It's about what you do with those gifts and that capability. A mechanic with extremely expensive tools might still do shoddy work, while a mechanic using the tool set her dad gave her might take more time and do a far better job. The difference is care.

Last summer I took my son on a five-day camping trip with a bunch of neighborhood friends. I unexpectedly had to leave early. Asa, who was eleven at the time, asked if he could stay. He really wanted to go rock jumping into the lake, which was the plan for the next day. At first, I was entirely against him staying to cruise the lake, jumping off rocks and whatnot.

Then Asa said, "Darren said I could stay with him." And that settled it for me. See, Darren is a great dad and a good friend. He's funny and clever and as creative a father as I've ever met. But it wasn't Darren's humor or talents that mattered to me in the moment. It was that he cared about my son. I knew he did. So Asa stayed for an extra day and night. He jumped off rocks and went mountain biking and built a fire and ate too many marshmallows. He had a great time. Asa told me all about it when Darren returned him to me, safe and happy.

I don't know who in your life is precious to you the way my son is to me. But think about that person for a moment and then think about who you'd be comfortable entrusting their safety and care to. Beloved, the list of people I'd leave my son in the woods with is really, *really* short. As it should be. Darren is on that list because I know, without question, that he'll take care of my boy.

I'd like to be on the list of people God trusts that way. I'd bet you'd like to be on God's list of care-takers as well.

Questions for Reflection

- What was your first job? How did it go?
- Do you have some limitations you *really* wish you didn't have?
- Who cares about you, and how do you know they care?

Chapter 4

FINDING MY STRIDE

or

FALLING IN LOVE (WITH WORK) IN MEXICO

'd like to tell you about the time I drooled on a man's shoes. I think it's time I told someone since I certainly didn't tell the man I drooled on.

I was on a flight home after spending a week in Mexicali, Mexico, with my friend Doug and a bunch of his high school friends. Doug was a youth pastor who had a long history of friendships in Mexicali, and once every summer, he'd escort a couple hundred students from the youth group he led to partner with his friends there. My primary role was to play music, leading Doug's high school friends in song during morning and evening sessions. Between those sessions, I got to drive around Mexicali with Doug and work alongside those same students as they repaired roofs, dug irrigation trenches, and did whatever was asked of them by the elders and leaders in that community. I also sat in on meetings and conversations Doug had with women and men he'd been partnering with for more than a decade.

Our days were full, overall. But it wasn't the posted schedule that wore me out to the point of drooling in public; it was that I didn't sleep during most of the time I was there. On the drive to the Mexico border from the East San Francisco Bay, a member of Doug's team asked if I was planning to join "Team Sleepless" that week. I told him I was up for whatever they had in mind, and he immediately responded by barking aloud to the rest of the fifteen-passenger van, "We got another one!"

Finding My Stride

Apparently, Doug went without much sleep for the five days he was in Mexicali. Instead, after the evening session, he would walk through the camp, ensuring kids had actually gone to sleep, and then he'd gather with whoever was still up to pray through the night. I'd definitely stayed up for days on end for lesser reasons. So I knew I could do it.

And I did.

For five days, my schedule was:

6:45–7:00 a.m. Organize song sheets and music gear

7:30 a.m. Sound check

8:00 a.m. Breakfast

8:30 a.m. Lead songs and facilitate the morning gathering

9:30 a.m. Depart camp with Doug to work with students and talk with community leaders

3:00 p.m. Return to camp

3:15 p.m. Fend off a nap

3:30 p.m. Fend off the desire to shower (because it made me want to nap)

5:00 p.m. Dinner

7:00 p.m. Organize song sheets and music gear

7:30 p.m. Lead songs and facilitate the evening gathering

9:00 p.m. Gather with Doug and the other members of Team Sleepless to debrief and then pray through the night

I. Had. So. Much. Fun.

I loved every minute of it.

But more than just enjoying my time, I felt very, very alive.

It's possible you've heard the St. Irenaeus expression: "The glory of God is a man fully alive." That was me that week. I was entirely in my element between music and conversation and even the physical labor (which I'd done very little of up to that point in my life but *really* enjoyed). That week was the closest I'd felt to anything resembling St. Irenaeus's expression, and it was the work I was doing that got me there. I don't think I would have articulated it quite this way at the time, but I know now that I was deeply and regularly connected to God and those around me.

I was also humbly and happily in touch with . . . myself? I was happy being me and not in some kind of ego-driven way; I liked who I must be in order to have been gifted such a special experience. I'd been to conferences and church services and other events designed specifically to elicit feelings of intimacy with the divine. And while I had appreciated or even enjoyed those gatherings (I sometimes still do), I hadn't experienced the kind of connectedness to God and others at any of those events the way I did on that five-day trip, leading songs and talking to kids and learning Spanish and slinging a hammer alongside Doug and his friends. That work connected me to God, myself, and those around me in a way that was utterly unique. I wanted more of it. It turns out, that's what God wants for me, too, which is why I'd been invited.

In his Gospel, Luke told a story in which Jesus, while he was walking in a crowd, was touched by a woman in that crowd, and instead of continuing on, he stopped to ask, "Who touched me?" Peter responded, "Master, the people are crowding and pressing against you" (8:45). In other words, there were a lot of folks touching Jesus as he walked along that road. Peter seemed surprised and even a bit confused that Jesus would have noticed one person's touch in particular. But for Jesus, there was clearly something very different about the connection he felt with that person. So not only did he notice that "power has gone out from me" (v. 46), but he also stopped to pay attention to someone in that crowd who would have gone entirely unnoticed otherwise.

> I was also humbly and happily in touch with . . . myself? I was happy being me and not in some kind of ego-driven way; I liked who I must be in order to have been gifted such a special experience.

Why?

I've heard a number of imaginative and inspiring explorations of what went on in Jesus' mind in this moment: that the woman who touched him wasn't entirely a stranger to him or that Jesus had a bit of an agenda to ensure women weren't constantly in the shadows. I think there's room for a number of such wonderings, and several can be true at the same time. So I'll add mine here. I think Jesus may have been uniquely moved by the depth and amount of power that went out from him because of the depth of that woman's need. Just as there's a particular depth of peace that comes with being well rested, there's a particular and unique joy that comes with being well spent.

> Just as there's a particular depth of peace that comes with being well rested, there's a particular and unique joy that comes with being well spent.

This woman who touched Jesus had lived for twelve years with the same physical condition, and she had spent all of her money on treatments that didn't work, including (I'd be willing to bet) a number of scams and swindlers. That's a heavy load to carry. I sincerely wonder if Jesus had a particularly gratifying reaction to being part of her Story—a Story he stopped long enough to listen to and become acquainted with, despite having somewhere else to be. I think, in shorthand, that might come off as cheap: Jesus liked being there and doing that work.

For months and even years, I looked back on my trip to Mexicali for the same reason; I liked how I felt doing it. I'd done a good number of jobs, but this was profoundly different.

Finding My Stride

In Mexicali, I'd done the kind of work in which I was fully alive and in tune with the Love of God. And not just the Love of God for me. Also the Love of God for my world and for my colaborers. Was I useful on that trip? Sure. But what was offered to me by God sounded less like *You'll be good with these tasks* and something more like *Come join me here. I want you to feel what I feel when you work with me.*

> What was offered to me by God sounded less like *You'll be good with these tasks* and something more like *Come join me here. I want you to feel what I feel when you work with me.*

Doug knew what he was doing when he invited me. Having worked with him before, I knew he valued my talents. But Doug had come to like me as a person as well. Inviting me on that trip was a way to share the goodness and Love of God with me. His invitation alone was an act of love, an extension of the Love of God in him. It meant I got to do the kind of work that would draw me deeper into relationship with God, with my world, and with my own soul . . .

the kind of work that deepens my love for the world I live in,

the kind of work that inspires care and awe for my colaborers, and also

the kind of work I'm happy to give the whole of my best energies to.

Good work (action) has provided me the sense of "aliveness" in ways that contemplation (in prayer or silence or just about any form of devotion) simply does not. It's not a superior or even deeper connection, per se; it's just vastly different and my soul longs for it.

Good work (action) has provided me the sense of "aliveness" in ways that contemplation (in prayer or silence or just about any form of devotion) simply does not.

So . . . about that drool . . .

After several nights without sleep, I didn't start to feel tired until the last thirty minutes of the three-hour drive from our campsite to the San Diego airport. Carrying my backpack and guitar through the terminal was a bit of a task, and by the time I got on the plane to Oakland, my body and mind were in full agreement that it was time to say goodbye to all other aspects of corporeal reality for a while. Which is when I sat down in the lounge section of the plane.

That's right, there was a lounge.

That didn't mean I was fancy. It just meant I was on a Southwest flight in the early-to-mid-'90s. The plane I boarded was a Boeing 737, and at that time Southwest had organized one set of seats on that particular 737 (the N95SW) like it was a Denny's. Six travelers on those planes would fly while face-to-face with other travelers.

Now, it's one thing to travel that way if you're with a business associate, and y'all have work things to talk about. Or if you're traveling with a friend you're comfortable staring at for two hours. But imagine the person across from you is a complete stranger. Then take that a step further and imagine if that complete stranger hadn't slept or showered for a few days and fell asleep slumped over so that he drooled on your shoes. Let's be honest: I might be some small part of why Southwest Airlines doesn't have lounge seating anymore.

I woke up midflight, wiped my mouth, and considered apologizing to the well-dressed businessperson across from me. It wasn't a lot of drool. But maybe, at that point, it didn't matter how much drool it was so much as it matters that we're talking about drool at all.

I didn't tell him.

Maybe I should have.

But I didn't.

In part because I couldn't think of a way to strike up that conversation without embarrassing myself. Also, I just hoped he wouldn't notice. But more than anything, I didn't apologize because I fell asleep almost immediately after sitting upright in my seat.

I. Was. So. Tired.

The thing is, I was happy to be so tired. I knew where my

energy had gone, and I felt really good about it. Let's think of it like that, shall we? Those droplets of drool were like little drips of joy, and I had blessed that man's feet with them.

I drove home in my 1992 Honda Civic Hatchback and slept through the night with a huge smile on my face (while, I assume, drooling freely onto my own pillow). I didn't feel any kind of anxiousness or guilt about my need for sleep. I wasn't thinking about what other work might need my attention. I just received the gift of rest as freely and deeply as I'd received the work of that week.

Remember what Parker Palmer wrote in *The Active Life* about contemplation and action both being rooted in our "ceaseless drive to be fully alive?"[1] Well, part of what I've learned is that being fully alive isn't just about being well rested. Sometimes it's about being well spent. More than that, Belovedness isn't a static reality. It is a lived, embodied, and practiced reality. Part of who you are as God's Beloved is capable and strong. You are not Beloved *so that* you can go do the work your soul desires to do. You are not "allowed" by Belovedness to go spend yourself if you just agree to return for a fill-up. You are Beloved fully and completely in and through the work you do

> Being fully alive isn't just about being well rested. Sometimes it's about being well spent. More than that, Belovedness isn't a static reality. It is a lived, embodied, and practiced reality.

with your own hands. You are called into that work so that you can know and live in that love.

Questions for Reflection

- What kind of work or project gives you a sense of God's nearness and love?
- Conversely, what kind of work leaves you feeling drained or distant from God?
- How much time do you spend doing one versus the other?

Chapter 5

PACING MYSELF

or

COFFEE, COLLEGE, AND
KNOWING MY LIMITS

To the best of my recollection, I only made two friends in college. I could be wrong about that number. It might have been as many as four. I felt too overwhelmed by my schedule to keep an accurate count. Besides the two folks I can remember spending time with, I also developed a somewhat intimate relationship with Coffee. Coffee became a friend because Coffee understood that I needed to be moving relentlessly and furiously in order to do as much as I was doing. I would say things like "Okay, Coffee. We've got three papers due this week, a wedding in Oregon, and we're taking kids to camp on Friday night." And Coffee would say, *Yes! Let's do all of these things and also a few others! Here are some ideas!*

I know a good number of people who enjoyed the social aspect of college. I just didn't. I was literally that person who wasn't there to make friends. Now, that doesn't mean I was rude about it; I was friendly. I just didn't say yes to many invitations. Also, and of note, I didn't get all that many invitations to social events. I think I got probably three. Maybe it was four. I don't remember. I was busy.

The schedule Coffee and I kept varied slightly from day to day, but not much. For instance, the average Thursday my senior year looked like this:

6:30 a.m. Wake up

Pacing Myself

7:15 a.m. Drive to class

8:00–9:30 a.m. Class

9:45–11(ish) a.m. Class

12:00 p.m. Drive to Clayton Valley High School (where my youth ministry crew was)

12:35 p.m. On campus with students

1:00 p.m. Drive back to class

1:30–3:00 p.m. Class

3:00–3:15 p.m. Realize I had no girlfriend and be pretty okay with that

4:00–5(ish) p.m. Work meeting

5:30 p.m. Dinner (usually a burrito from a nearby taqueria)

5:30–6:30 p.m. Reading for classes over dinner

7:00–10:00 p.m. A class on monsters in movies

Now, I don't think I was unusual among college students for doing homework late at night. Pretty much everyone I knew at the time was working on papers and projects after 10 p.m. But a primary difference between me and a lot of those other students was that I didn't own a computer. I had to use my mom's

Macintosh LC 580, which was at her house and a good thirty-five to forty minutes from my college campus. It was quite the thrilling, single nightlife I had, rolling into my mom's pad at 11:30 p.m. to write about the relationship between Greek pottery and the Western religious obsession with the sky. (Yes, that's a paper I actually wrote. No, you can't read it.)

Which brings me to the night in question.

It was a Thursday night, and my paper was due Friday morning. I was clacking away on the keyboard, and my heart was singing with joy as my paper's thesis became clear and I neared a reasonable, if not beautiful, conclusion. My heart was also beating somewhat quickly, which I took slight notice of but didn't think much about. That is, until I noticed the pinky and ring fingers on my left hand felt numb on the keyboard. When I pressed down, the tips of those fingers didn't register the keys.

That kinda freaked me out.

And by "kinda," I kinda mean "completely."

Obsessing over other tics or oddities in my body, I noticed my skin felt sticky and that my breathing was a bit fast. I could tell my heart was racing, so I asked Coffee if he had any idea what was going on. *I don't know, man. But I'm here with you. It's gonna be okay.*

The next thing I knew, the same fingers on my right hand were also numb. So I did the very thing you'd expect a reasonable and levelheaded person to do in such a moment: I called my doctor to tell him I was dying.

Like I said, I kinda freaked out.

Now, you might have heard someone say something like "I thought I was dying" before. And when you did, you knew they were intentionally exaggerating. But let me assure you, not only was I open to the idea that I might be nearing my end in that moment, but those were the exact words I used in my voice message.

I made that call just after 4 a.m. And as much as dying seemed like a huge bummer, I had a paper due. So Coffee and I got back to work. Somewhere near 4:45 a.m., Dr. Davidson called back.

"Hey there, Justin. Listen, I don't think you're dying, but you should definitely come in. The office doesn't open until seven, but I'll be there by six. Why don't you meet me then?"

I printed out my paper, which was "mostly done," as they say in academic circles, and headed to Dr. Davidson's office. He checked my blood pressure and heart rate and listened to my breathing. He then checked the dilation of my eyes and made me say "aah" with the wooden tongue depressor. Finally, he stepped back, looked at me for a moment, and said, "You aren't dying, but . . ." which is such a strange way to deliver such good news. I mean, while I'm not a doctor, I'd like to think that, if I were a doctor and I got to tell someone they weren't dying, I'd probably give that tidbit of information a good minute or so to settle in before introducing any caveats or "buts." That's not how Dr. Davidson played it, though.

"You aren't dying, *but* . . . can I ask you about how much coffee you're drinking these days?"

"Not that much," I said, suddenly aware of how orange my thirty-two-ounce travel mug was.

"Let's walk through your day yesterday. Start in the morning. Did you make coffee at home?"

It only took a few minutes for me to recount my schedule to him, this time including Coffee.

> **6:30 a.m.** Wake up (made coffee with my roommate and I think I had two cups)

> **7:15 a.m.** Drive to class (grabbed a coffee along the way)

> **8:00–9:30 a.m.** Class (I left class once to get coffee at the café on campus)

> (I got coffee between classes)

> **9:45–11(ish) a.m.** Class (I left class again to get coffee at that same café on campus)

> **12:00 p.m.** Drive to Clayton Valley High School (where my youth ministry crew was)

12:35 p.m. On campus with students (grabbed a coffee with students on campus)

1:00 p.m. Drive back to class (grabbed a coffee for lunch)

1:30–3:00 p.m. Class (I left class again to get coffee at that same café on campus)

3:00–3:15 p.m. Realize I have no girlfriend and be pretty okay with that

4:00–5(ish) p.m. Work meeting (at a coffee shop)

5:30 p.m. Dinner (at the nearby taqueria, which is next door to a coffee shop, so . . .)

5:30–6:30 p.m. Reading for classes over dinner (I drink coffee while I read)

7:00–10:00 p.m. A class on monsters in movies (the professor knows we're wiped out, so he makes coffee for class)

Dr. Davidson scratched at the pad of paper he was holding. "That's about sixteen cups of coffee. Do you think that sounds like a lot?"

I sipped my coffee while considering his question. "I do think that sounds like a bit much."

"Yes, Justin. It is."

I took another sip and nodded.

"Well, the way I see it, you're at somewhat of a crossroads, young man. You can either taper off your caffeine consumption or move on to something more like speed." I was tempted to ask how much speed might cost and if he knew a guy. I didn't. I wasn't sure if he'd be legally required to report me, and I didn't want to go to jail; I had too much to do.

In all seriousness, what Dr. Davidson was pointing out was that, while that level of consumption was a bit extreme for one day, it was far worse because it had become normal. A lot of my days looked like that, and Coffee played that same role on a lot of those days. More importantly and more deeply, he was challenging me about the way I had chosen to respond to my limitations.

I had come to think of my limitations as obstacles and was growing dependent on chemicals not just to deal with them but even to eliminate them. By working to overcome or bypass my limitations, I was, in effect, declaring that my humanity was in the way of my productivity; it was a problem that I was human.

A few years ago, Motorola ran a commercial for a phone called the Droid 2. Maybe you've seen it. In the commercial a youngish man is seated at a boardroom table listening to a presentation when his phone, the new Droid 2, goes off on the desk in front of him. He's been sent a complicated schematic. Glancing around the table to see if anyone is watching, he picks up the device and quickly looks over the image. He then begins typing very, very quickly. As he does, his fingers, wrists, and forearms morph from human tissue and bone into steel and wire and blinking lights; he becomes part machine. Finally, having read the message and responded, he puts down the phone and offers his attention back to the presenter. The commercial's narrator wraps up the thirty-second spot, saying, "Turning you into an instrument of efficiency . . . introducing the new Droid 2 by Motorola."[1]

That tagline is a short way of saying something like:

In order to do what needs to be done, you need to be other than (and better than) you are. You have to be less limited. You have to be less human. If you can't attend to two to four things at the same time and with equal focus and effectiveness, that's a problem. If you can't be two places at once, that's also a problem. If you can't maintain the same intensity of work energy and focus over the course of a day or week, that's a problem. If you regularly get tired, that's a really big problem. There are only twenty-four hours in a day, and there's so much work to do! What can be done to help you overcome your very limited nature so that you can be a better piece of the machine?

That narrative and the voice that speaks it are part of what Jesus was warning people about when he said, "The thief comes only to steal and kill and destroy" (John 10:10). It is a very real voice and a very real force that can be very convincing.

It leverages our interests and passions, appealing to our altruism and care. Ultimately that voice suggests that if we want to be part of something bigger than ourselves (which we all do), we'll have to become better and more efficient instruments and tools. But becoming an efficient instrument isn't the invitation of the God who loves you.

"I have come that they may have life, and have it to the full," Jesus continued.

The invitation Jesus makes isn't specifically about work. Nor is it specifically about rest. The invitation Jesus makes is to be *fully alive* and *fully loved* by God in both work and rest. Absolutely, being a Beloved of God's means sharing in God's loving work in the world you and I live in. But far from stopping there, being a Beloved of God's also means that my drive or motivation to work and my freedom to fully rest are extensions of and celebrations of God's love.

> Being a Beloved of God's also means that my drive or motivation to work and my freedom to fully rest are extensions of and celebrations of God's love. That's the full life.

That's the full life.

That's the life I want for you.

Maybe you're like me in that I would not have come to a knowledge of my physical and emotional limitations as clearly had I not packed my schedule full and pushed myself to my ends. So I'm actually quite glad I did. Sincerely, I am. Because once

I hit my limits, I was faced with the question, "What will you do about this?"

I needed to actually face that question before I started to answer it. For a long season (many years, in fact), my answer was not "Having run up against my limitations, I will learn to rest in the goodness of God, whose gifts make my work possible." Instead, my answer was "Having run up against my limitations, I will pump myself full of chemicals and try to overcome them." And because I am Beloved, I got to live in the long, grace-filled learning curve of being wrong about myself. It took quite a few moments like the one with Dr. Davidson before I started hearing God say, *There's more to the full life than you are seeing right now. I'd like to show you more and then give it to you.*

Can I give myself wholeheartedly to work that lights me up and makes me happy? Yes! And so can you. Because God's love runs deeper than ours, and we join God in it when we work.

Can I set down my agenda and even my hopes and dreams and just rest? Yes! And so can you. Because God's love runs deeper than ours, and we join God in it when we Sabbath.

Questions for Reflection

- What do you lean on or depend on when you're up against your limits?
- What do you give yourself to wholeheartedly?
- Do you ever feel like you don't deserve to rest?

Chapter 6

RUNNING WITH OTHERS

or

NINETY POUNDS OF
RICE AND MAKING
LASTING FRIENDSHIPS

On May 15 of last year, I ran in a race in San Francisco called the "Bay to Breakers." It's one of my favorite runs in the country for a few reasons, including the fact that many of those who run the race do it in costume. This year, I ran the full 15k (about nine miles) in a zebra pajama onesie. For the first bit of the race, I was the only zebra around. But when I got to mile six, I spotted a runner ahead wearing the exact same onesie! I picked up the pace a bit and eventually caught him, only to find out my zebra twin was running alongside a giraffe, a panda, and a unicorn! We all slowed down enough to talk and laugh together for about a mile and a half. Turns out, we were all parents of kids under ten, who were now sweating through their kids' pajamas. It's not every day I get to run alongside a bunch of adults who are also wearing animal pajamas. In fact, I only get to do that once I'm running the race.

I think that's a somewhat accurate picture of what it looks like to find and make true friends. I can't just pick folks at random or watch people from a distance and hope things will work out or that our lives will pair well. I have to be running my race at my pace and then look up to see who's with me and who I'm with.

> I can't just pick folks at random or watch people from a distance and hope things will work out or that our lives will pair well.

Running with Others

For a good portion of the time when I was on Young Life staff, I was pulling in somewhere between $650 to $800 per month. It was tough to pay for rent, gas, and food with only that much coming in. Thankfully, my roommate, Stavros, and I had a ninety-pound sack of rice.

Please ask me how we acquired a ninety-pound sack of rice.

We got the rice from a guy named Don, who had been a faithful supporter of the organization for many years. He had a reputation for cheerful, spontaneous generosity. So when he approached my roommate and me during the annual golf tournament fundraiser, we knew it was a really big deal.

We had been running sodas and waters to golfers in the clubhouse when Don got up from his table to intercept us. He said he'd heard about the work we were doing with kids, and he was proud of us. "I'd like to support you guys."

This is it! I thought. *This guy is about to write us a huge check!*

He asked us to follow him outside. In my mind, that had to mean he was about to write us a check *so big* he didn't want to write it in front of other people. Don kept chatting about his history with Young Life as we weaved through cars in the parking lot. When we finally reached his car, Don unlocked and lifted his trunk. I thought that seemed like a weird place to keep a checkbook. So maybe it wasn't a check? Maybe he was going to give us cash! *That makes sense now! We're going to be handed a suitcase full of cash!* I started to imagine Stav and myself racing through the streets of Concord, California, dodging the web of spies and international interlopers who were also after Don's suitcase of cash.

How thrilling!

But (and you saw this coming, right?) there wasn't a check, and there wasn't a suitcase of cash. Instead, Don opened his trunk to reveal an enormous burlap sack, which took up almost the entire trunk. And because my mind was abuzz with confusion, I could only really make out one word.

". . . rice."

Don smiled and casually gestured toward the sack of rice, saying, "I've had this in the garage for a long time, and I thought you'd like to have it."

Let's pause here for a moment to take stock of a few things.

1. That's a lot of rice. I weighed about 155 pounds at the time, meaning that sack of rice was a spoiled lap dog away from being my size.

2. We didn't have a way to make rice and, shortly after being gifted the rice, had to purchase a rice cooker.

3. If you have to buy something in order to enjoy a gift you've been given, you kinda got ripped off.

4. I don't feel like I needed to know the rice was really old, and I'm not sure why he told us that part.

Regardless, we loaded the ninety pounds of rice into my 1992 Honda Civic Hatchback and headed home.

We had rice every day for close to one year. I mean, we changed it up, of course. Sometimes it was rice with soup. Sometimes it was rice with yesterday's soup. Sometimes it was even rice with yesterday's rice. Our recipes were relatively few, but we kept them in steady rotation. To be entirely honest, we really liked how simple it made things not to think or worry about what we were going to eat. It felt a little bit like living into the teaching Jesus gave about worry: "Therefore I tell you, do not worry about your life, what you will eat or drink; or about your body, what you will wear. Is not life more than food, and the body more than clothes?" (Matthew 6:25).

I know there might be a few ways to apply that teaching. So I'm glad I found myself running alongside someone who, just as quickly as I did, was able to apply ninety pounds of rice to it. Let's be honest here: not everybody would be pleased to simplify their diet to old grains. But that was us!

Now, don't get me wrong; we definitely got tired of rice at times and enjoyed mixing in the occasional PB&J. But having that particular item checked off of the to-do list meant Stavros and I could focus on what we wanted to be doing with our time, which was ministering to kids and spending time with people we liked, including each other. And that's the thing about the rice gift for which I'm most thankful: It helped me see and enjoy the rare gift I had, not just in my job but in the people I was doing that job with. Specifically my roommate, Stavros.

You've likely heard it said or sung that "Good love is hard to find."[1] I think that's true of far more than just romantic love. The older I get, the more I think it's harder to find good friendships than anything else. One of the most common questions I get from young adults on retreats is about finding and developing healthy, life-giving friendships. In those conversations, I've come to say something like this:

If you want to live arm in arm with solid people who share your values, don't chase friendship. Instead, choose good, meaningful work, and work hard at it. Then look up and see who's running in the same direction and at your pace.

If I want to really know what someone cares about and what they value, I look at how they're spending their time and energy. What are they doing that sets their heart on fire? That isn't always their job. Sometimes, someone's job is the thing that supports their *real* life's work. And even then, if you want to know what someone is really about, look for what lights them up from head to toe.

Sometimes, someone's job is the thing that supports their *real* life's work. And even then, if you want to know what someone is really about, look for what lights them up from head to toe.

Jesus told a parable at one point about a man who finds a treasure in a field, saying:

> "The kingdom of heaven is like treasure hidden in a field. When a man found it, he hid it again, and then in his joy went and sold all he had and bought that field.
>
> "Again, the kingdom of heaven is like a merchant looking for fine pearls. When he found one of great value, he went away and sold everything he had and bought it." (Matthew 13:44–46)

When I started working with Young Life, I quite literally sold just about everything I owned, including my bed! For about two years, I slept on a small floor mat in a subzero sleeping bag from REI because I liked what I'd found in this job and liked what I saw in myself while I was doing it, even though I knew it wasn't going to pay much. Meanwhile, I looked up from that mat on the floor to see my roommate doing the same thing— sacrificing time and resources other people in their twenties were chasing so that he could be available to kids at a local school.

How good might it feel to know, without question, that you share the values and interests of the person you're spending time with? How might some of your friendships be enriched and clarified by doing meaningful work together?

During a recent Q&A session, I was asked if I thought Jesus had an active social life. I'm guessing he did. What I get to know about Jesus' friendships is that he spent most of his thirties with twelve to twenty people who were very in tune with his mission. Those are the stories we get to be familiar with. I'd also be willing to bet there were hijinks and adventures well beyond what is written in the public accounts. I'd venture to guess Jesus and his friends might have enjoyed some equivalent to hopping the golf course fence with snorkels and swimsuits to collect golf balls from the pond on hole sixteen so that they could use the nearly one hundred balls they collected to invent games for their friends (yes, we did that, and goodness was it fun!). The responsible risk-taking and spirit of adventure that marked our work life translated quite naturally into our social escapades.

Which reminds me. There was this one night . . .

I was late coming home after work. We'd planned on making dinner that night, but it turned out Stav was late getting home as well, which was evident the moment I walked in. Sure enough, Stav was prepping dinner, stirring older rice into newer rice. But he was doing so while wearing fishing waders, a wrestling singlet, goggles, and one of those beanie hats with a propeller on top. He'd been playing games with kids that night too. I didn't say a word about his choice of clothing but instead went to my closet to retrieve a full-body jumpsuit I'd made entirely of duct tape.

Halfway through dinner, one of us said something like "Look at us; all dressed up with nowhere to go."

On one hand, that was true. Neither of us was dating anyone (and dressed like that, can you imagine why?), so going out to meet girls was pretty much off the table. Regardless, we went with the inspiration.

Running with Others

"Eh, let's just head out and see what happens."

We'd been driving around for about fifteen minutes when one of us said, "Honestly, dressed like this, I kinda wish there was a carnival in town." And that's when we saw the luminous glow in the not-too-distant distance.

Yes.

You guessed it.

A carnival.

It was as if God had heard us wishing out loud and said, *Hey! That's a good idea!* And just plopped one down on the other side of town for us to discover.

We drove through the parking lot to the employee entrance, where we were waved in by the security guard. Mostly, he just looked at us like he knew us as we drove past him. For the next couple of hours, we walked around the carnival like we owned the place, taking pictures with kids and collecting a few tips along the way.

I think we left with close to two hundred dollars.

Meaningful work put me in proximity to some priceless, like-minded friends—friends with whom I lived out some of the greatest, most enjoyable adventures of my life. Friends who also shared in some of the hardest parts of being alive, including the loss of my father and the cruel loss of life among the high school students I was leading and caring for. The thing is, I had to be *doing work that was close to my heart* in order for that to be true. Yes, I had to learn to do that work at a pace at which I could notice the people around me, but I wasn't going to slow my pace to notice those people until the people were there. And, at least in my story, it was the work that drew us together.

Truth is, especially at that phase of my life, I'm pretty sure I didn't know what was truly meaningful to me, much less have the ability to articulate it. That is, not until I had to make actual decisions about how I wanted to live. Part of what gets clarified in work is the shape of your own heart. You get to discover what it is you actually care about and what you're best at by trying. Sure, you might be wrong, but you'll never really know that until you've put in the work.

Insofar as I was willing to sleep on the floor and eat rice every day, helping kids get to know God must have been pretty meaningful to me. I'm positive I would not have come to that knowledge by just having conversations about "calling" or by reading a textbook about vocation. For my part, the choices I had to make in order to do the work I wanted to do exposed and highlighted those values in me. Then, once I could see them, I was able to recognize those same values in someone else.

Nowadays, I know how much I value creativity in leadership and in art and in ministry and entrepreneurship. Not just because I think it makes for more beautiful works in those cultural spaces but because I think that a posture and practice of creativity forges a connection between people and God that isn't as easily or clearly available otherwise. I know I want to see people who are leading in those cultural spaces live more freely and deeply connected to God, so I'm making the choices I need to make in order to do that work. When I look up, I see myself running alongside women and men who share that value, and I'm very excited about the friends I get to share the second half of my life with.

> If you want to live arm in arm with solid people who share your values, don't chase friendship. Instead, choose good, meaningful work and work hard at it. Then look up and see who is running in the same direction and at your pace.

Meanwhile Stavros and I are still friends. Our families will go camping together again this summer. And then there's this: twenty-five years after Stavros and I met on Young Life staff, my twelve-year-old son will head to a Young Life camp with a group of kids that includes Stavros's twelve-year-old daughter.

It's worth repeating:

If you want to live arm in arm with solid people who share your values, don't chase friendship. Instead, choose good, meaningful work and work hard at it. Then look up and see who is running in the same direction and at your pace.

Questions for Reflection

- Do you connect with and enjoy the people you currently work with or around?
- Do you ever feel lonely or alone? What do you do about it?
- What lights you up from head to toe? Does anybody share that with you?
- What do you consider "meaningful"? Some might say "child hunger," and some might say "education." What kind of work strikes you as meaningful?

Chapter 7

TRIPPING OVER MYSELF

or

THE WORST SNOW TRIP EVER AND DISCOVERING I AM THE GIFT

'll be forty-nine when this book is published, and I've started joking with friends and family that, in light of the biblical instructions regarding the Jubilee year, that means all the gifts I've ever given to them have to come back to me. In all honesty, I've given some pretty undesirable gifts over the years, including the year my roommate and I found one hundred mini Slinky walking spiral toys in a dumpster. Merry Christmas, everybody! I'm glad I'm joking. Not about finding the Slinkys—about wanting them back.

What I am serious about regarding my forty-ninth birthday, though, is that I don't want anyone to buy me gifts. I mean, I won't be unkind about it, and I'll thankfully accept some taco socks if someone hands me a pair, but all I will want for my birthday is to spend time with people I like and love and with people who like and love me. People are the gift I want as well as the gift God truly desires to give.

Most of the kids who showed up to my Young Life club couldn't cover the cost of trips we planned. I didn't want them missing out, so I'd spend the money I'd saved by eating rice every day to ensure they could get places. The summer before their junior year of high school, six boys signed up for a camping trip. When the time came to turn in the $150 deposit, none of them had it. So I asked a few donors to help me come up with nine hundred dollars. Between their help and a few dollars I made selling some golf balls back to the driving range I'd lifted them from, we were able to cover that cost.

Of the twenty to thirty regulars, there were only three or four girls in the mix, partly because my leadership team was mostly made up of me, myself, and I. The other reason there were so few girls showing up was because those boys were very "boy-ish." And yes, I mean all the things you might think I mean when I say that, from farts to fart jokes to a general lack of decorum (and often deodorant).

Of those three or four girls, I was most thankful for Leah. She skateboarded as well as most of the boys (almost everyone showing up to Wednesday night club was a good skater) and regularly outwitted the room when things got snarky. For the record, things always got snarky. Leah was consistent and faithful and attended pretty much everything. In fact, she was the only girl to sign up for the one and only ski trip I ever planned. I'm really glad she went. Not glad enough to plan another ski trip. But glad I get to tell you this story.

There were fourteen boys on the trip and then Leah. I had to ask my friend Sara to come on the trip so Leah could go with a non-male leader. Sara agreed to chaperone as long as I promised to "not leave her alone with those disgusting boys." We had a deal.

After the three-hour drive, my crew and I hiked through the dark and up the snowy hill about thirty yards to the cabin, where we heaped our snow gear, sleeping bags, and pillows in a huge pile in the middle of the living room floor. Then, literally every one of them stepped back outside to smoke. Every one of them. Now, I really wish they didn't smoke. I'm not a fan of smoking at all. But I've gotta be honest and tell you I was impressed at their commitment to that particular addiction. It was twenty degrees outside! It was even colder when, after dinner, they all went *back* outside for *another* cigarette. This time, they were only outside for about ten minutes before a kid named Mike came rushing back in, out of breath.

"Hey, um . . . someone's in the woods outside."

Sure enough, as I stood on the deck outside waving the smoke out of my eyes, I could see what appeared to be a herd of bison moving toward the lodge. They weren't bison, of course; they were football players. Another Young Life leader named Grant had *also* booked the same cabin that weekend and brought with him twenty massive guys from East Palo Alto. As they walked through the front door, I'm almost certain I felt the cabin tilt.

Once everyone was in from the cold, Grant set his hand on my shoulder and said, "Well, it appears we've got ourselves a bit of a dilemma, eh?" Between high school students and leaders, there were now thirty-nine people in a cabin with only twenty beds. "Ya know what?" I said. "I can fix this. We can just sleep downstairs. Right, guys?"

Nobody replied. They'd all gone back outside to smoke.

Sleeping downstairs was a decent plan, and, in the end, that's exactly what we ended up doing. Here was the thing, though:

There wasn't really a "downstairs." I mean, there were stairs, sure. But when you picture a "downstairs" you might picture things like carpeting and walls dividing rooms with doors on hinges and stuff like that. We didn't find those things when we got downstairs. We found ourselves surrounded by the 2x4 framing of what might, in the future, become rooms. There wasn't even drywall over the framing. The only walls with any covering were the outer walls, which, as it turned out, hadn't been insulated.

Mike spoke up again, saying, "We're gonna die down here."

To which someone responded, "Nah, we aren't gonna die. We'll probably just freeze, and scientists will find us in a couple hundred years to wake us back up."

I ran back upstairs to grab the three small space heaters we'd seen in the hall closet, giving two to the boys and one to Leah and Sara. Then I lay down in the space between those two spaces to mark a clear delineation between "Boys' area" and "Leah's room."

It wasn't the cold that kept me up that night (although that didn't help). It also wasn't the grumbling and complaining I heard off and on (though that didn't help either). What really kept me up until dawn was the pitfall of emotions in me about how badly I'd failed these kids and how weak a leader I was.

The next morning, right after breakfast, Grant asked if we'd like to join him and his crew for what he called their "morning conversation," a way to set a meaningful tone for the day by asking a few questions and talking about matters of soul-level significance. Part of me really admired him for this and how he was really with it as a leader. Another part of me was envious and a little bit irked. Something like *Great. One more way I've clearly blown it for these kids. I was just planning to eat, pack up, and go to the mountain. I didn't have any kind of "meaningful" thing planned at all.*

After my crew took their post-breakfast smoke break, we gathered in the living room. My crew globbed together on one side while Grant's army sat on the other. It looked like a snapshot of a Looney Tunes cartoon in which the scrawny Bugs Bunny and his motley crew face off against an *actual* sports team. Grant started by asking what people would ask God if they could have a meeting and ask just one question. Peter, one of my crew, immediately raised his hand and said, "I'd want to know what God's farts smell like."

OhdearLordpleasemakeitstop . . .

But it didn't stop. Grant just smiled, seemingly unphased, and kept asking questions, stirring conversation, mainly among his crew. They said things like "I'd want to know why my grandma had to die" and "Why isn't there enough food for everyone?" Once the conversation got rolling, it became clear that Grant's club wasn't just physically larger; they were spiritually and emotionally more articulate. I felt like a fake and that everyone could see it. After Peter's initial crack about divine flatulence, my crew was pretty much a squirming mass of giggles and whispers. I kept hoping the fire alarm would go off or that World War III would break out. Anything to keep my ragtag group of miscreants from getting called on again. I really didn't want them talking aloud and exposing me.

But Grant really was a wiser and more insightful leader than I was in that moment. (He still is, to be honest. Grant has become a dear friend and a trusted mentor. I learn from him every single time I'm around him.) So instead of avoiding the smoking section, he turned to face them directly and said, "I haven't heard much from this group. Can I ask you a question?"

A few of them shrugged, which is as close to a "yes" as they offered in response to just about anything besides "Do you have a light?"

"Why do you come to Young Life club?" Grant asked. "What's in it for you? Why did you come on this trip?" My mouth dried up like I'd eaten a down pillow. After a long moment of silence, Leah spoke up. "I think I speak for all of us when I say I just like being around Justin."

I didn't see that coming.

It wasn't an ego boost *at all.* I wasn't feeling good about my work or abilities right then and would not have believed someone who said, "Justin, you're doing such a good job!" No, this was something quite different. It was a heavenly truth breaking into my life in a way I could not have planned for and probably wouldn't have received otherwise—that regardless of my skill level or execution, I was what God was giving these kids. It wasn't just my talent or strength or the opportunities I could offer. It was me.

There is a kind of spiritual knowledge I've only ever come to by putting the best I have into something, failing at it, and then finding people on the other side of my "failure" who happily point at the goodness they see in me. It's like writing checks for people so that they'll value me, discovering there isn't money enough in my account to make the checks worth anything, and then finding out those folks weren't there to pick up a check; they were actually there because they wanted to be.

I don't know if I can theologically get behind the idea that God set me up to be double-booked in that cabin with the Tongan national weightlifting team, but I can definitely see God prompting Leah to say what I needed to hear when I was actually ready to receive it. And what it seemed God wanted me to hear was something like

> It's not ultimately about what you offer or what you provide. It's about who you are in offering and providing those things. The gifts and experiences you bring to the table are like celery with peanut butter on it. The celery is just a delivery method. You're the peanut butter.

I really loved those kids. A lot. I didn't want anything they lacked (or thought they lacked) to keep them from knowing how endlessly and relentlessly loved they were. All the while, I was learning something very similar about myself, something I needed a little help seeing. Not only was I loved in the same way I wanted those kids to be, but it was, in fact, my Belovedness I was passing on. Knowing myself the way I do now, I can say with confidence that I wasn't going to pray or meditate myself to a functional, embodied version of that knowledge. I had to feel it in me and see it played out in real life. It was in and through work I learned I was the gift God was offering.

Thank God Grant asked that question. And thank God Leah saw past my job to the person I was while I did it. In fact, thank God I "dropped the ball" and double-booked that cabin and spent the night feeling like a failure. Because I'm pretty sure I wouldn't have come to see myself as Beloved if those things hadn't happened.

I can't imagine having learned it any other way.

Questions for Reflection

- What's the best gift you've ever received?
- Who might consider you to be a gift? Why do you think that person feels that way?
- What person do you consider to be a gift? Why do you feel that way about him or her?

Chapter 8

TAKING A BREATHER

or

EXHAUSTION ISN'T
PROFESSIONAL

Somewhere around 2008, and after nearly a decade on tour supporting me as a singer-songwriter, in rental cars or on buses, my wife was feeling the effects of "road life." In search of resources to help her clarify the experience she was having with exhaustion and overwork, she came across a short excerpt from Mark Buchanan's book entitled *The Rest of God: Restoring Your Soul by Restoring Sabbath*.[1]

The conversation we had after she read the excerpt went roughly like this:

> **Amy.** This seems like it could be helpful for us right now.
> **Me.** Sounds great. Can you summarize it?
> **Amy.** It's an excerpt. You want me to summarize the excerpt?
> **Me.** Yes please. I'm between things and have a moment. Go ahead.
> **Amy.** I think you should just take the five minutes to read it.
> **Me.** I really don't have that kind of time.

This might be a few words off, but it's pretty accurate. It's also a solid representation of my mindset at the time. I wasn't dismissive of rest, specifically; I was dismissive of anything that wasn't already on my plate or directly related to my job. I had established myself as a professional musician now, and I was convinced that meant a new and deeper level of commitment to the job. A Sabbath practice sounded very much like an addition to what I already had going on. It wasn't that I found myself above the need for rest; it was that I didn't clearly and easily (or quickly) see how resting might make me a better worker.

> I wasn't dismissive of rest, specifically; I was dismissive of anything that wasn't already on my plate or directly related to my job.

I didn't read the excerpt. You saw that coming. My wife, on the other hand, ordered the book and read it, which led to a follow-up conversation.

Amy. I think this book is speaking pretty directly to where we are right now.

Me. Cool. Can you summarize it?

Amy. You could read the excerpt I sent to you.

Me. I don't know where that is, actually. How about you tell me what the actionables are. Is there a bottom line?

Amy. Well, for one thing, we should be taking days off.

Me. I hear that, and it sounds really great. I can't imagine how I'd pull that off.

I turned my computer monitor toward Amy to gesture at the fullness of my weeks. Quite literally, I had events or travel planned every weekend for almost two months before there was a break in the schedule at all.

Amy pointed at the first open weekend and said, "What about this Saturday? Let's block that out and take that day off."

"Sure thing."

To be entirely honest, I only agreed to her plan because I thought it was the quickest way to finish the conversation so I could get back to work. Not only that, but you can tell how unseriously I meant yes when, just a few days later, I received a gig offer for that same weekend to which I *also* said yes.

> **Me.** I'm really sorry to do this, but I won't be around on that Saturday. I just took a weekend gig in Kansas City. I'll be at Heartland Community Church for the weekend.
>
> **Amy.** What's it for? What's the weekend about?
>
> **Me.** I don't really know. I'll email Dan to find out.

As it turned out, pastor Dan Deeble and the Heartland staff had just read Mark Buchanan's *The Rest of God*, and I was being invited there for the weekend they'd be focusing on the book as a whole church body. Dan told me he'd send me a copy of the book, which he did. Which meant I now had two unread copies of it at home. Both of which would remain unread in the weeks leading up to that trip. Well, that's not entirely true. I read the back of the book and a few paragraphs from the final chapter so that I could get the gist of it and do the job. That's the way my prayer and devotional life were working at the time; I wanted to get just enough to keep me energized and focused for my work.

I arrived a few weeks later in Kansas City, energized enough to do the job while being wholly uninformed. But it wasn't my lack of knowledge about the book or the practice of Sabbath that stood out to my friend Dan. It was how tired I was.

Taking a Breather

On the Sunday of that weekend, I was helping lead music during their gatherings, and at some point Dan pulled me aside. "Man, you seem really worn out." I didn't deny it or act like I didn't know. Instead, I did something considerably more insidious; I wrote it off.

"Yeah, well, I've got a lot going on between music and this book project I've started. I've also started helping to lead a local church. You know how it is, all part of being a professional, right?"

Dan tilted his head slightly and shrugged. "I dunno. I mean, I get being busy, but I don't think that means you have to be exhausted. You don't seem like yourself. May I make a suggestion?"

Dan proposed I stay in town for a couple of days instead of heading directly home. He'd cover the cost of changing my ticket and would put me up in a place where I could relax and rest and actually practice some of what we'd been preaching over the weekend.

"I even have a book for you to read," he said. At which point (you guessed it), he handed me Mark Buchanan's book entitled *The Rest of God: Restoring Your Soul by Restoring Sabbath.*

Later that afternoon, while I was packing up my gear and getting ready to head to the retreat house Dan set up for me, I received a text from a friend in Nashville.

"Are you available this week?"

"Yes I am."

"Can you get here by tomorrow afternoon?"

"Yes I can."

And just like that, I booked myself a gig in Nashville, meaning I'd be ditching Dan's offer to help me get some rest.

> **Dan.** What's the gig?
> **Me.** I don't really know. I think it's a retreat since he asked if I could be around for a few days.

Dan was gracious with me, though I could tell he was clearly disappointed. "Let me know how it goes. Also, let me know what it is when you find out!"

It wasn't until I was walking onto the plane that I got through to my friend in Nashville to ask more specific questions about the gig I just took.

"It's a two-day retreat for artists, and the song leader we hired can't make it. I didn't want to ask someone in town since the retreat is for them. How fortunate that you're already out this way!"

"Agreed! So, what's the focus of the retreat? I'll start preparing songs and readings on the flight over."

"We brought in an author named Mark Buchanan. He just released a book entitled *The Rest of God: Restoring Your Soul by Restoring Sabbath*. Have you heard about it?"

"Yes . . . yes I have."

"Awesome! He'll be leading the sessions and focusing on rest."

Oh.

My.

Goodness.

Now, this story would be bonkers enough if it ended there. But there's more to it. Because when I walked in the door of the retreat facility, the song leader they'd originally hired was already in the room and all set up.

"I never said I wasn't coming. I'm not sure why they called you. Sorry, man."

So there I was in Nashville, with nothing to do but to sit in a retreat with the man whose book had been chasing me around the country.

During the first part of the first session, Mark Buchanan, author of the book *The Rest of God: Restoring Your Soul by Restoring Sabbath* and leader of the retreat God had suckered me into attending, said, "I'm going to assume you all love your job. I want to suggest that if you want to continue to love your job, you have to learn to not do it."

Beginning with that sentence, Mark spent the next few minutes dismantling one of the most wrongheaded and destructive ideas I held about what it meant to be committed to my career—that being a professional meant being exhausted. Turns out, being tired all the time isn't a sign of professionalism any more than being injured is a sign of athletic prowess. For someone calling themselves a "professional," exhaustion is a sign that something needs to change.

> Being tired all the time isn't a sign of professionalism any more than being injured is a sign of athletic prowess. For someone calling themselves a "professional," exhaustion is a sign that something needs to change.

I'd adopted the idea that a professional pushed through tiredness and even burnout because he was "more committed" to getting the job done than "unprofessional" people. But if we go back to the parallel with athletics, one of the differences between elite professional athletes and amateur athletes is endurance. And while some of that has to do with being in better shape, a lot of it has to do with knowing one's mental and physical capacities and pacing oneself for the duration of a game, season, or even a whole career.

In his book *The War of Art: Break Through the Blocks and*

Taking a Breather

Win Your Inner Creative Battles, Steven Pressfield uses that same comparison:

> The professional arms himself with patience, not only to give the stars time to align in his career, but to keep himself from flaming out in each individual work. He knows that any job, whether it's a novel or a kitchen remodel, takes twice as long as he thinks and costs twice as much. . . . The professional steels himself at the start of a project, reminding himself it is the Iditarod, not the sixty-yard dash.[2]

Of course, working hard *is* part of professional life. When it's time to put in the extra hours, I can joyfully do that. But being a professional also means knowing my limits in loving wisdom so that, when all that extra work and extra effort is not doing the trick, I feel the freedom to take a step back. It means knowing that I don't want to "flame out" in this work because there's more at hand than just the project I'm on. And I don't just mean "the next project after this one." I mean something much deeper.

> Working hard is part of professional life. When it's time to put in the extra hours, I can joyfully do that. But being a professional also means knowing my limits in loving wisdom so that, when all that extra work and extra effort is not doing the trick, I feel the freedom to take a step back.

Parker Palmer says in his

book *The Active Life: A Spirituality of Work, Creativity, and Caring,*

> The word *professional* originally had a very different meaning. At root, a professional is *one who makes a profession of faith*—faith in something larger and wiser than his or her own powers. . . . The true professional is a person whose action points beyond his or her self to that underlying reality, that hidden wholeness, on which we can all rely.[3]

What I profess when I give the best of myself to the work I've chosen is that I have seen something so deeply good and beautiful and true of God that I respond by offering the best of my time and energy. Not because there's a bottom line I want to add to, but because I want to share in and be part of God's love for the world. What I long to profess in and through my work is that I am drawn into the Story of God by the Love of God.

I live just about forty minutes from the Golden Gate Bridge. The American Society of Civil Engineers considers the bridge one of the "Marvels of the Modern World."[4] One of the reasons that is the case, along with its architectural beauty, is that *only* ten people died during its construction. At the time it was built, in 1933, the expectation was that, for every million dollars it took to finish a major construction project, one worker's life would be lost. The Golden Gate Bridge cost roughly $35 million to build, meaning the cost of human life was one-third the standard. Compare that to twenty-seven people who died during the construction of the Brooklyn Bridge,[5] nearly one hundred who died while building the Hoover Dam,[6] and a mind-boggling twenty-five thousand people who died while building the Panama Canal.[7] The loss of human life was routinely factored into the cost of major projects. The common sentiment seems to have been "People are *going to die,* but it's worth it to get the job done." I don't like the story that kind of thinking tells. So I don't want to make that profession. I want to say something far better.

That's what my friend Dan wanted for me when I saw him in Kansas City. He was being the better professional. Dan looked at me and, although I was doing my job well, was paying attention to the person I was while I was doing it. That's what mattered to him. He pointed beyond and through the job to my Belovedness and then professed that Belovedness by extending the offer of rest to me.

In the process of writing this very book, I made the decision to push back an early deadline. That basically amounts to telling the publisher "I won't have this done when I told you I would." I didn't like saying that at all. But after almost two years of navigating COVID-related travel restrictions, event shutdowns, and somewhat seismic shifts in consumer attitudes toward the arts, I wasn't in a clear enough or healthy enough place to make this book what I wanted it to be.

Could I have pushed through and put in the hours, probably late at night, to get it done? Maybe. Well, probably. I've definitely done that before. But I don't like what it would have cost me mentally, emotionally, and physically. I also don't like what it would have cost my kids (not just in the amount of time I'd have had available to them but also in the quality of that time when I had it). So I talked with my team at HarperCollins Christian Publishing, and we set a new date that would allow me to finish the book in a pattern of health. In turn, I get to offer you the fruit of a more whole pattern of my life, one rooted in Belovedness rather than one simply committed to getting the job done.

I like the story that decision tells. And I want you to be able to tell those same kinds of stories about your work. I think that is the "professional" thing to do.

Questions for Reflection

- Have you been told that you seem tired? How did you respond?
- In your mind, what makes a good professional?
- In light of the definition I used for the word *professional*, what do you want your work to say?

Chapter 9

RUNNING HURT

or

CROOKED IN GERMANY
AND THE GIFT OF REST

Have you ever dealt with a bad case of jet lag? Yikes. It's terribly disorienting. Thankfully, most of my travel over the years has been within the continental United States. That's not to say it doesn't feel odd to leave Atlanta at 2 p.m., fly for five hours, and land in San Francisco only to find that it's 4 p.m.

I have at times traveled internationally, which can be a full-blown head trip. The flight from San Francisco to Frankfurt, Germany, is right at about eleven hours. What makes the trip hard isn't the time on the plane so much as it is my internal clock (still on Martinez, California, time) being way out of whack with the clocks in the Frankfurt terminal.

On my first trip to Germany, I struggled for the first two days to stay awake. So for the second trip, I had a plan. My plan was to stay up all night before my trip and then sleep the entire flight. When I woke up in Frankfurt, it'd be ten o'clock in the morning there, and I'd be all set! So that's what I did. When I boarded the plane and climbed into my window seat, it was "Bye-bye, consciousness! See ya in Europe!"

When I woke up in Germany, my brain felt rested and refreshed. It worked! My back felt a little weird, but I figured that'd pass. I felt a little tweak when I stood up. I'd slept with my head and neck a bit crooked and one leg bent upward a bit. So I thought that once I got moving things would loosen up.

That plan was also working as I made my way through the airport—until I lifted my fifty-five-pound "I'm going to Europe" backpack onto my shoulders. At this point, that weird feeling became more like a stab, but I still assumed the pain would pass as I kept moving and loosening my back. Of course, anywhere *I* went, my heavy backpack went too. Instead of my back loosening up, it went into something like lockdown mode. And for the next three days, I was in excruciating pain.

I had to take long breaks while walking, and it hurt to breathe. It would take me several minutes to get up out of a chair and even longer to get out of bed. For two days, I was a mess. On the third day, my trip host saw me wince while I lifted the strap of my guitar over my head and said, "We need to get you checked out. I'll call the chiropractor." The chiropractor he referred me to was working on the army base in Heidelberg. Most of the trip had me visiting army bases in Würzburg, Kaiserslautern, and now Heidelberg. Seeing an army doctor wasn't the most comforting thought. I was suddenly imagining myself doing jumping jacks while being barked at by Gunnery Sergeant Hartman from *Full Metal Jacket*: "You want me to adjust that back, son? *Adjust that attitude first!*"

That's not at all what happened.

It turned out the chiropractor on base was a Canadian named Sara. She didn't yell at me once during the hour I was there. Instead, she asked me to be very quiet and relax while she slowly tugged at my heels and wrists. This wasn't the "snap, crackle, pop" kind of chiropractic practice I was familiar with (mainly from movies). It was a longer, quieter, and more involved process. By the time I stood up, I could do so without pain and even felt a bit taller (which I might have been!).

During part of my hour with Sara the Canadian chiropractor, she asked me how I ended up that way. I told her, "I think it's because I slept kinda funny." By which I meant I'd pretzeled myself against an airplane window for eleven hours.

"Yeah, you definitely slept wrong."

And isn't that a strange sentence.

Not every kind of "rest" is the same. Just as there are ways to work and ways not to work, rest can be done in ways that won't provide what our minds and bodies need. In fact, resting improperly can actually cause us problems.

"Wait," you might be asking. "I can rest too much? Or rest in the wrong way?"

I think so, yeah. I think we can rest in a way that means we end up crooked and in pain, physically, mentally, and emotionally.

Not every kind of "rest" is the same. Just as there are ways to work and ways not to work, rest can be done in ways that won't provide what our minds and bodies need. In fact, resting improperly can actually cause us problems.

Aside from my ridiculous example from Germany, I can think of a few ways I've gone about rest in less than helpful ways.

The first way I've rested poorly is *resting so I can get back to work*.

There have been long seasons in my life during which I've made a tool out of rest—a tool dedicated entirely to ensuring I stay in working shape. And insofar as "resting" that way is all about making me a better worker, I'm not treating myself like a whole, Beloved person, am I? Meanwhile, it's very likely that thinking of and treating myself like a piece of machinery is a big part of why I feel so tired all the time. Resting so I can get back to work is just a way to mask the problem while not coming close to addressing the actual problem. In fact, it reinforces and supports the narrative that is beating me up, that I'm supposed to be useful at all costs! When I've been exhausted and realizing I need rest, the real problem has been that I'm treating myself like a tool of industry rather than God's Beloved. Part of what I'm saying when I'm resting so I can get back to work is that I'm okay being treated like machinery as long as I can be a productive and efficient part of that machinery. That's gross.

> When I've been exhausted and realizing I need rest, the real problem has been that I'm treating myself like a tool of industry rather than God's Beloved.

Second, I've also treated *rest as a reward for work*.

I'm actually comfortable with resting as a reward on occasion and in small ways. In other words, saying, "I'm going to get this thing done and then take the fattest nap ever!" is definitely something I've done, and that nap was, in fact, the fattest one ever. But I'll confess that when I've lived and worked this way for weeks or months on end, as a pattern, my work has suffered pretty badly. I've written elsewhere about projects I worked on this way and then had to go back to fix because I'd put so many tired, scattered, and unfocused hours into them. Once I had completed the project and then taken a break (during which I got a touch of rest), I came back with a slightly clearer mind to find myself embarrassed at how bad things were. Not only did that result in having functionally wasted hours and days (and sometimes weeks) of precious work time, but it meant having to now add *more* work hours to the project. That's silly.

Third, I have also tried *resting infrequently or sporadically.*

What I've learned is that, in the same way that working out *really hard* every once in a while will never counteract the effects of regularly eating garbage and living sedentarily, so resting every once in a while doesn't help me become healthy. In other words, it's not eating fast food on occasion that's the problem; it's eating a lot of fast food and doing it regularly. The problem isn't that I slouch when I sit in a particular chair or when I'm tired; it's when I'm slouching all the time and won't sit up straight no matter how many times my mom tells me to! It's not having one drink that's the problem; it's when that drink happens every day or several times a day.

It's the pattern.

It's the practice.

And the only real cure for unhealthy patterns is creating better, more human patterns. That's it. There isn't another way.

My friend Matt works with baseball and softball players, mainly working on their hitting. He can watch a player swing a bat a few times (sometimes even just once) and immediately tell them why they aren't hitting as consistently or as hard as they could be. He will also tell you that fixing or improving a batter's swing doesn't happen in one, two, or even three coaching sessions. That player has probably been swinging the same way for years, and those movements are locked into her mind and her body. The change happens when, after having those few sessions and trusting the instruction she gets from Coach Lisle, an athlete makes a regular practice of swinging her bat differently. If that new practice doesn't happen, a new and better swing is nothing but a neat idea she picked up at a clinic. It's *practice* that changes things.

Keep in mind that a significant part of what true rest does is help us detox from the patterns that wear us out and malform our souls. Plugging in a random day off on occasion or even spontaneously can actually feel pretty bad. Why? Because just like that athlete's body is used to her former swing, so your soul is used to certain patterns and postures, even if they're unhealthy. And there's a comfort that comes with familiarity, even familiarity with bad habits, that can keep us in bad spots.

That is, until we practice enough to get familiar with and comfortable with the new.

If the work I'm doing is actually sucking the life out of me, just "getting away" every once in a while doesn't help me figure out *why* that is or how it might change. In other words, maybe I really do need to change my job. Or maybe I need to just change a few things about how I do my job. But it can be hard to tell what's really wrong without the proper attitude and perspective. That means making the time to think through things in detail. Most of life's wisdom doesn't come in a flash; it comes with time and caring attention. Infrequent breaks don't give me that. A regular practice of rest does.

> Most of life's wisdom doesn't come in a flash; it comes with time and caring attention. Infrequent breaks don't give me that. A regular practice of rest does.

The fourth way I know to rest poorly is to become "vacation dependent."

I know "I need a vacation" is a thing people say. I've heard it in movies and in regular conversation. I may have even said it myself. But I've come to believe at this point that vacations and leisure trips are worth far more and can be more restorative (and far more enjoyable) in the context of a life in which rest is a regular practice. Consider how many people you know come back from a long-awaited vacation and immediately wish they had a few days of vacation to recover from their vacation! Or maybe they half-jokingly suggest they need a separate vacation from the work it took to make the vacation happen.

> If my soul doesn't know what it feels like to rest, time away from work can very easily become another form of work. I just won't use the time well because I don't know how.

If my soul doesn't know what it feels like to rest, time away from work can very easily become another form of work. I just won't use the time well because I don't know how. I book the hotels, secure the rentals and the plane tickets, pay the resort fees, and manage the details for seven to fourteen days—only to come home wiped out and feeling like time flew by without my experiencing it.

A reliance on vacations can distort my relationship with everyday life too. Maybe you've heard people talk about how badly they wished they lived in Hawaii or Tahiti or Tahoe or wherever it is they "get away." As much as I understand that sentiment, it's also a dismissal of the goodness available right where we live. "Home" becomes a place where things get done, while "fun" and "happiness" are on a beach a thousand miles away. That's a terrible way to live.

A dependency on vacation can also malform my relationship to work. I can end up thinking of "work" as a thing I have to do but am mostly just happy getting away from. Work becomes a necessary evil, while "vacation" becomes the hero and the antidote.

In his book *The Icarus Deception: How High Will You Fly?*, Seth Godin tells a story about being on a trip to some beautiful spot in the world where folks travel for vacation and leisure. He's sitting in the lobby of his hotel, working on a laptop, when he overhears someone at the table next to him talking about how sad it is that Seth is working on his vacation. He responds by remarking how sad it is to have a job you need to get away from.[1]

Too many people return from an escapist vacation adventure to their regular patterns of work and home with a deeper resentment for daily life. All of that is to the detriment of the loved ones and projects and organizations they'd joyfully given themselves to at some earlier point. I hope our departure from our normal patterns can lead to a renewed love and joy for the life we *get* to live. Too often, in the absence of a regular pattern of rest, "vacations" steal that everyday joy.

> I hope our departure from our normal patterns can lead to a renewed love and joy for the life we *get* to live. Too often, in the absence of a regular pattern of rest, "vacations" steal that everyday joy.

A regular Sabbath helps to counteract the relentless and ruthless drumbeat of the other narratives that would seek to enslave me.

A regular Sabbath means having enough rest often enough that it affects (and infects) the days around it. I'm not just breaking from work; I'm intentionally touching base with God, the Source of my Belovedness, so that I can learn to see and experience that same sense of wholeness in the entirety of my life. Finding joy and life in my everyday begins with being able to recognize joy and life to begin with. The regularity of a weekly Sabbath trains my eye to see that way right where I am.

The proximity of a Sabbath practice (in that it happens in direct and regular relationship to my everyday relationships and circumstances) helps to clear my vision to see more completely and lovingly what I have.

As it turns out, one of the reasons jet lag knocks people out as hard as it does is that our bodies and minds are so tired already that we don't have the ability to recover quickly from the disorientation. Which is to say, instead of staying up all night so I could sleep all morning and arrive in Germany with my head on straight, I needed to become a generally better-rested person.

I'm working on it. Join me?

Questions for Reflection

- Have you ever had jet lag? What was that like?
- Do you have a regular practice of rest? Is it weekly? Monthly?
- What helps you feel truly rested?

Chapter 10

QUITTING THE RACE "FOR GOOD"

or

DISCONNECT AND REPAIR

I am not the most tech-savvy person I know, but I'm also not a Neanderthal. I can be helpful when my mom needs help figuring out why her computer and printer aren't syncing, and I can make my way around the operating system of the laptop I'm currently using.

The thing is, most of my tech knowledge hasn't come because I'm computer smart. It has come from having to deal with a wild array of problems. At one point, a lizard somehow crawled inside my desktop and died, shorting out a few cables that made my monitor act funny. About a year later, I had to have my laptop cleaned out because a spider had laid eggs in my keyboard. I couldn't type the letters *J*, *N*, or *M* for a few days and couldn't figure out why. It turns out those three letters were home to quite a few baby spiders!

I've heard the question "Have you tried turning it off and back on?" more than once. And while I know it's mostly used as a joke nowadays, I also know rebooting works! And not just with our devices. I think it works pretty consistently for our brains and bodies.

For instance, I wear a simple Bluetooth headset (the Treblab XR500) when I jog or go to the gym. I don't sweat to the oldies, as it were, but I do prefer listening to music or, more often than that, an audiobook when I'm doing fitness stuff. Truth be told, before Bluetooth technology, I used to be the guy you'd see in the gym with a paperback book. "Read 'n' Lift" was kinda my thing. Now I'm just one more guy in the gym with a headset. That's not to say I've abandoned my Read 'n' Lift program altogether. You might look across the weight room to find me doing hang squat cleans and think I'm blaring Rage Against the Machine. Instead, it's probably Julia Cameron saying, "Growth is an erratic forward movement: two steps forward, one step back"[1] or the words of Henri Nouwen: "The mystery of one man is too immense and too profound to be explained by another man."[2] Of course, on occasion you'd be right that it's Rage. I try to keep myself guessing.

If you're like me, your phone keeps a list of Bluetooth devices it has been connected to so that, if and when I am in range of that device, the connection is easier to make. Also if you're like me, that list can get a bit long. Right now, my phone's Bluetooth list features twelve possible devices, including one named "78:2B:64:8E:22:92." I have no idea what that is or how it got on the list, but I'm hoping it means I'm connected to a satellite somewhere over the Arctic that can beam the next Josh Ritter album directly into space.

Because I connect to more than one Bluetooth device with my phone, I have to reconnect to my Treblab headset every time I go back to use it. As you probably know, that can sometimes be a tricky procedure. Maybe you've been there, clicking back and forth between devices and having to turn Bluetooth off entirely and then back on. Then turn the headset off and back on, all the while saying something like "Why don't you just connect?" Sometimes we're dealing with Bluetooth interference because of physical objects between devices. Sometimes it's because there are other electrical messages moving around the same space, and those signals can show up like static in your ears. Apparently this happens with microwaves a lot. Which is just weird to me. I mean, what on earth could your microwave have to say, and why is it trying to get through to you?

Another key reason a Bluetooth device will randomly disconnect is that it is competing for a limited space on the available spectrum. These devices are capable of transferring only a certain amount of data packets to a certain number of other devices. The frequencies on which these communications happen can get really crowded, like a roadway or a water pipe. At which point, it becomes necessary to limit the number of available pairings, which limits the number of data packets on the spectrum, hopefully ensuring a cleaner, smoother connection.

So it is with you and me. At some point, it becomes clear that, in light of all the connections we've forged and all the data being passed back and forth in those connections, we've come up against or even exceeded our capacity to connect clearly. At that point, just like we have to do with our devices, it becomes necessary to limit the number of connections we're trying to maintain.

In my experience, the hardest part of that process is looking at my list of connections and discerning which ones are more important and which ones are peripheral. I want to do all the things all the time and have all the conversations with all the people. I want to maintain all my connections! I just can't. In

117

> Some connections really are more important than others. A regular practice of Sabbath rest has been key to figuring out which ones are which. The process can be hard.

large part because trying to do everything all the time eventually distorts and interferes with my important connections. And maybe that sounds as harsh to you as it did to me when I started realizing it. But it's true, nonetheless. Some connections really are more important than others. A regular practice of Sabbath rest has been key to figuring out which ones are which. The process can be hard. It can also be really, really sad.

When I started practicing a weekly Sabbath, I struggled with what to do and not do. Buchanan's book *The Rest of God: Restoring Your Soul by Restoring Sabbath* helped me discover this very simple mantra about Sabbath day practices:

Cease from what is necessary.

Embrace that which gives life.

And then do whatever you want.[3]

It was a clever way to simplify what had, up to that point, been a confusing and overcomplicated conversation. But as simple as that mantra is, the challenge it offered me was considerable. I'd never even thought about distinguishing my joys from my obligations. I'd just come to consider joy something I picked up along the way while I was doing the things I was supposed to do.

So I cracked open my journal and made two lists: "Obligations" and "Joys." As I started filling spaces in each category, I realized two things almost immediately. First, I didn't easily know the difference between the emotional rewards of doing good work for God and the pure joy that came from just being loved by God. That took a while to start seeing, and the process is ongoing. The other thing I realized pretty early was that I needed to take a hard look at the way I experienced my relationships.

On the second or third round of making those two lists, I wrote the words *mentorship/counseling* on my "Obligations" list. Here's the problem with that: It wasn't actually what was in my mind when I wrote it. What was really in my mind was that, while I sincerely enjoyed the parts of my job that required me to mentor and counsel, pretty much all my relationships were that way; I was almost always on the giving side of the exchange. I didn't seem to have many relationships in which I was just me and loved for it. I was in most of my relationships because I was useful and helpful.

When I thought about *things* that simply brought me joy without feeling obligated to them, I thought about hiking and reading comics. But when I thought about *people* with whom I experienced that kind of simple joy, my mind went blank. Who would I spend time with if my hope was to feel cared for instead of just useful? Filled up instead of just helpful? That was a really, really short list.

Quitting the Race "For Good"

I was coming to see that I experienced almost all my relationships as obligatory work, whether or not those people were on my calendar as clients, gathered with me on Sundays as congregants, or living around the corner as neighbors. This was a sad realization.

It was an equally sad realization when I came to notice that, in a lot of cases, it wasn't just my learned posture or desire to perform that left me feeling isolated. Most of my connections were *set up* to be one-sided. I was often invited places because I was considered funny or entertaining or maybe even knowledgeable; I was useful and helpful. I know I'm hardly alone in this experience among my vocational peers. Artists can feel "used" quite often. And the numbers tell a tough story about the loneliness of people in full-time vocational ministry.

Research by the Duke Divinity School Clergy Health Initiative[4] suggests that a majority of ministers feel they don't have a close friend. And that's just the folks who had the courage and self-awareness to admit it! Don't get me wrong; I really liked being useful. That's why I was willing to agree to a social structure that was almost exclusively predicated on the use of my strengths and talents. But boy was it a bummer to feel like I'd set myself up with so few places to feel personally valued. I needed more than a break. I needed somehow to forget what I knew about relationships.

Fast-forward to a few weeks ago when I set out for the long run I take almost every week. Part of my current Sabbath practice is giving myself time to run and not worrying about having to cut it off because I have somewhere to be. On the Sabbath, I get to run until I'm done. That feels amazing. Stepping onto the trailhead, I went to pair my Bluetooth headset to my phone so I could listen to the audiobook I'd just picked up. But they wouldn't pair. I did all the things I mentioned above. I turned off both the phone and the headset and then tried getting the devices to sync again. They wouldn't. It was like brokering a compromise between hungry toddlers (or entitled members of the United States House of Representatives).

Finally, thumbing over the options in my phone's settings, the iOS prompted me to "forget this connection." I'd never seen that before. I clicked the red text and the name Treblab XR500 disappeared from the menu. A few moments later, I reconnected the headset to my phone as if it were a brand-new connection. And I got to spend the next hour or so on the trail, just me and Priya Parker.

There comes a point when a connection is so rife with bad memories, bad habits, or bad patterns that it's just not enough to get some distance or take a break. We have to somehow forget. We need to get our soul to stop thinking, feeling, acting, and reacting the way it has. This can take a very, very long time. But more than forgetting, it actually takes remembering something better and truer about ourselves.

One of the things folks in recovery have taught me is that a key to ending addictive patterns is the creation of new and better patterns. No, that doesn't mean I replace one addiction with another addiction; it just means I realize that I chase the thing I'm addicted to (be it prestige or pleasure or a sense of being useful) by doing certain things. So if you're trying to get sober, the nights and times you'd normally go to the bar to drink with people (or sit alone in your place to drink by yourself), you'd go to AA meetings or movies or ball games with people who want you sober and whole.

There's something very real about what happens when we "turn our eyes upon Jesus," not just as an idea but as a practice. There's a gift and power available to us when we let ourselves see and *be seen* regularly by The Face of Perfect Love.

That's the thing about redemptive and loving self-knowledge: it's not a static piece of data like the ones being transferred between devices over Bluetooth. It's practiced and lived knowledge, formed into your soul less like clay in the hands of some power you've given yourself to and more like the set of muscles that grow and strengthen under the guidance of a good coach. So you can look into the mirror and *tell* yourself you're valuable in and of yourself, but if you build a life where the majority of your connections are ones in which you're being used, that knowledge too easily becomes the kind of sentiment found on birthday cards (which hang out for a day before ending up in the trash or recycling bin).

It's likely you're familiar with some of the lyrics from Helen H. Lemmel's oft-sung hymn "Turn Your Eyes Upon Jesus." The ones from the chorus ring in my soul.

8

Turn your eyes upon Jesus

Look full in his wonderful face

And the things of earth will grow strangely dim

In the light of his glory and grace[5]

Look, I know it's "just a song." And I know the imagery in that song can be over-romanticized at times. But I'm telling you there's something to that for me, and I'm betting the same is true for you. There's something very real about what happens when we "turn our eyes upon Jesus," not just as an idea but as a practice. There's a gift and power available to us when we let ourselves see and *be seen* regularly by The Face of Perfect Love.

> Sabbath practice gave me the chance to hear and see and feel and know that while it may always be true that I am predominately useful to the majority of people, I am fundamentally and immovably Beloved by the One Who Holds My Life Together.

As you start to remember your own Belovedness, you also start to forget being seen any other way. Being Beloved isn't just an alternative story to the one in which we are predominately useful; it's what's most deeply true of us. And here's the thing about truth: once my soul gets used to it, other things don't just sound like "other things"; they sound wrong. Because they are.

Quitting the Race "For Good"

Just as a regular Sabbath practice gave me the opportunity to recognize something really hard about my life's social structure—namely, that a lot of it was predicated on my utility or usefulness—so that same Sabbath practice gave me the chance to hear and see and feel and know that while it may always be true that I am predominately useful to the majority of people, I am fundamentally and immovably Beloved by the One Who Holds My Life Together.

So are you.

O soul, are you weary and troubled?

No light in the darkness you see?

There's light for a look at the Savior

And life more abundant and free[6]

Questions for Reflection

- Do you feel like you're sending and receiving a lot of "data"? Maybe too much?
- Are there connections you'd like to "forget" in the way I described?
- What would it look like for you to reset?

Chapter 11

BEING A FRONT-RUNNER

or

TRUE COMPASSION AND LEARNING TO LEAD WITH LOVE

In the spring of 2000, I toured as the opening act for a band that included a moment during their set to advocate for children living in poverty. At some point in the evening, the show would stop and one of the band members would share a story. Usually it was a story about their experience with child sponsorship. Then they'd invite (or sometimes even challenge) their audience to also sponsor a child.

I liked a lot about that element each night. I liked the storytelling part quite a bit (shocking, I know). The stories the band told were different from their other storytelling moments, which were usually intended to set up a song. These stories about their sponsored children had a different weight to them, something more human. More than anything, I liked that people who showed up for songs and stories left having decided to invest in another person's life.

That was the toughest adjustment to life on the road—missing people's everyday ups and downs and life changes. I'd spent the previous years as a Young Life leader and church planter, sharing in the struggles and victories of people I knew, liked, and cared for. I got to see wholesale change happen in those lives over time. Touring meant showing up in Baton Rouge on Tuesday afternoon, playing some songs, telling some stories, and then leaving later that night, hoping to God something I said or sang made a lasting difference.

So when I started playing more shows on my own, I took a cue from that band I'd opened for and started traveling with child sponsorship packets. I loved knowing that kids in Quito, Ecuador, were getting education, food, and medicine because a twenty-year-old college student decided to spend her time and money investing in an even younger life. But the thing that really got to me was what might happen in the heart of that college student. I was moved by the hope that a seed of generosity and charity might sprout and grow in that young adult. Who knows what it might grow into?

I visited Quito during that first year as an advocate, and my heart, like the Grinch's, grew three sizes. I didn't feel like a hero or savior at all, which I know is a critique of some who go on such trips. Instead, if I felt "privileged" at all, I felt privileged to be any part of the lives of these brilliant young people and what God was doing in, through, and among them.

I also started looking at my time, talent, and money very differently. I felt clearer about my priorities and freer from some of the consumer patterns that had ensnared me. Coming home to hit the road again, I wanted people like me to share in what I'd experienced and to live more fully because of it.

When I started my work in advocacy, somewhere close to 50 percent of the earth's population lived on less than a dollar per day, and most of those people were children. Somewhere around twenty thousand kids died every day because they didn't have access to clean drinking water or food. Over time, the urgency of the matter crept to the forefront of my advocacy. There was so much work to do, and all of it was very important because there were lives on the line. I did the job a lot and was starting to "get good" at it.

In the summer of 2006, I was invited by Compassion International to be a speaker and advocate at the Cornerstone Festival in Illinois. My job there was twofold. On the one hand, I'd get to tell the stories I'd collected about child sponsorship and invite people to become sponsors themselves. On the other hand, I was also going to be the Main Stage emcee. In theory, that meant I'd get to introduce Main Stage bands and entertain the audience between acts. Of course, that was all predicated on my ability to entertain the Main Stage audience at the 2006 Cornerstone Festival.

Here's what I found out: I was not able to entertain the Main Stage audience at the 2006 Cornerstone Festival.

At one point, as I walked onto the stage, someone yelled, "Oh, crap! It's the guy who wastes our time while we're not listening to the bands!" I was bad at the emcee job. I was so bad, in fact, that when it was time for me to change gears and invite that crowd to consider joining the effort to rescue children from poverty, that same crowd responded by hurling objects at me.

At first it was just trash—cans and bottles and a few food wrappers. I did everything I could think of (besides leaving the stage altogether) to recapture the moment. Nothing worked. The boos kept coming, and so did random objects from the annoyed and impatient crowd. The frenzied energy kept building until I was hit in the face with what must have been about two dollars in change. I winced and stumbled back to discover a few quarters and dimes on the stage in front of me and a small drop of blood on my left brow. "That hurt," I said into the microphone. The boos and jeers stopped for a moment.

Then, as the anger in me took hold, I said things I wish I hadn't said, regardless of how effective they might have been. "So let me get this straight: you're more willing to throw money at me to get me to stop talking about these kids than you would be willing to give that same amount of money to save one of their lives? Is that really who you are? Is that really who you want to be?"

Among the many things the Compassion team and I talked about while debriefing the disaster, I was told, in no uncertain terms, that heaping that kind of guilt on people was not in the Compassion International Speaker Advocacy Handbook.

A lot had gone wrong that weekend besides my calamitous reaction to the Main Stage audience. But the thing that became most clear to me came later that night when Jamie Tworkowski took the stage to represent To Write Love on Her Arms. If you're not familiar, TWLOHA provides resources and pathways for people (predominantly young people) who are struggling with depression, addiction, self-injury, and suicide. While Jamie spoke about how hard it can be to just be a kid and how valuable each of them is, the place was almost entirely still. And it wasn't just the stillness of respect; the majority of young faces were turned up with eyes fixed on Jamie, who was standing at the end of the catwalk. The way someone turns toward a familiar voice. The way that beloved disciple of Jesus must have turned toward him when he called her name on

Resurrection Morning. "Mary" (John 20:16). The Main Stage crowd was listening because they felt called by name. They felt loved.

I wasn't calling the names of the kids in the crowd, and that was the "piece I was missing," as it were. I was just trying to convince a crowd of persons of a certain age and demographic to do a thing I thought they should do because I knew it was important. And yes, it was a good thing and an important thing. But I'd allowed the urgency of my cause to change the way I saw the people in front of me. I wasn't seeing them as Beloved in their own right. I was seeing them as potentially useful in achieving the sponsorship goal.

Advocacy doesn't begin because God so dearly loves people living in poverty that He's willing to use people of means to solve the problem of poverty. That's a sad, mechanical way to think about people, and it makes the real problem worse. See, at its root, poverty erodes and strips away the essential value of a human life. It's not just that you don't have access to things that might bring you health or joy; it's that poverty says you must not be worthy of such things, otherwise you'd have them. And there I was, challenging the basic humanity of the people in front of me in order to convince them to "join the movement."

I didn't love the people in the crowd that day.

I didn't even really care about them.

And they could feel it.

And more than anything else, that is why they didn't respond to my "invitation."

In what I find to be one of the strangest and most confounding moments in Jesus' Story, he walked a few of his disciples to the top of a mountain, started glowing, and, while he was glowing, had a short conversation with two long-dead heroes of the Jewish faith. This moment is generally called the Transfiguration. In his Gospel, Matthew recorded it like this:

> After six days Jesus took with him Peter, James and John the brother of James, and led them up a high mountain by themselves. There he was transfigured before them. His face shone like the sun, and his clothes became as white as the light. Just then there appeared before them Moses and Elijah, talking with Jesus.
>
> Peter said to Jesus, "Lord, it is good for us to be here. If you wish, I will put up three shelters—one for you, one for Moses and one for Elijah."
>
> While he was still speaking, a bright cloud covered them, and a voice from the cloud said, "This is my Son, whom I love; with him I am well pleased. Listen to him!"
>
> When the disciples heard this, they fell facedown to the ground, terrified. But Jesus came and touched them. "Get up," he said. "Don't be afraid." When they looked up, they saw no one except Jesus. (17:1–8)

After seeing what I'd seen and experiencing what I'd experienced, I think I felt a lot like Peter. "Lord, it is good for us to be here. If you wish, I will put up three shelters—one for you, one for Moses and one for Elijah." In other words, *This seems important and urgent. I'd like to build something for it!* And that's not a bad impulse. In fact, it's a good one. But Peter missed the same thing I'd missed (or lost track of along the way). I don't think God was trying to "wow" Peter into action. I also don't think God was trying to convince Peter to get to work because of how serious God was about God's work. If I'm reading the moment right, God was inviting Peter into the Love he shared with Jesus. That's why, the moment Peter chimed in with his premature and urgent reaction, God said, "This is my Son, whom I love; with him I am well pleased. Listen to him!"

That's the invitation: *I love him. Listen to him!*

Not "Listen to him because great things will happen if you do" or even "Listen to him because this is really, really important." It's about the Love of God in, through, and for Jesus. God seemed to be saying something like *All this? It's about Belovedness. Yes, rest in it. Yes, work with me in it. But know all the while that it's not about what you do; it's about my love in, through, and for you. Don't miss that.*

Peter missed that.

So did I.

I don't want you to miss that.

On their way down the mountain, Jesus told his disciples not to say a word about what they'd seen (v. 9). I think that, at least in part, he knew they weren't ready to do anything about what they'd seen. Neither was I after what I'd seen and experienced in Ecuador. And maybe you're still chewing on something God gave to you or showed you. Maybe you need to take some time to know you weren't gifted that feeling or knowledge or experience *just* so you could pass it on. Maybe you need to receive it as a gift to you first. And then, after you've felt Loved by God in it, you can pass on the Love you've been given.

I don't know how many of those Beloved folks at Cornerstone decided to become sponsors that night. I hope and believe that, by God's good grace and abundant Love, beautiful things happened in and through those who did. What I know for sure is that there isn't a work or a task or a project in all the world more important to God than who you are when God calls you to it. And that if I don't know that to be true when I'm making the invitation, I'm a poor messenger.

Questions for Reflection

- Have you ever seen someone get booed onstage? How did they respond?
- Can you remember a time you felt used by someone you thought didn't care about you?
- Why do you think Jesus asked his disciples not to say anything about what they'd seen on the mountain?

Chapter 12

I'M NOT RUNNING TO "WIN"

or

TRADING YOUR SOUL FOR THE WORLD

s he serious? He can't be serious!"

That's what a participant at one of my Sabbath Keeping workshops had to say about me a few years ago. In short, he and I disagreed about the viability of a weekly rest day. And while I usually don't mind disagreement, things got complicated when, instead of hashing out his disagreement with me in person, this participant expressed his frustrations to the director of the organization who had hired me as a presenter.

In my formerly anxious work posture, I might have felt responsible for this man's reaction. I might have wanted to pursue a conversation with him (over email or phone) and try working through it so he could see what I was trying to say. I'd want to convince him. I'd want to fix it.

But I didn't.

In the years leading up to that moment, I'd practiced enough of what I was preaching that I was able to actually let go of my desire to be overly responsible for someone else's growth. Instead I chose to trust the process he was already in, a process held together by the One Who Holds All Things Together. After all, it wasn't *my* love and care I was trying to inject into his life, and it wasn't *my* wisdom I was trying to impart to him. I had finally realized that, because I was a Beloved One of God's,

I'm Not Running to "Win"

I had been invited to be part of the work God was already doing in that dear brother's life. Instead of feeling responsible to make something good happen for him, I recognized the privilege it was to share the ways God had been good to me while hoping that, by inspiration or challenge, I could help him see and embrace the existing work God was doing.

> Sabbath rest has changed me. I'd even go so far as to say that it has saved me. Having taken fifty-two workdays a year off the calendar, I've begun to hear the loving voice of God say, *Son, you can't do it all. Do the part you can; the rest is mine. Leave it to me.*

Now, this kind of thinking didn't come natural to me. To be honest, I like being in control. I also prefer knowing that I'm going to have the effect I intend to have when I work. The practice of Sabbath rest has changed me. I'd even go so far as to say that it has saved me. Having taken fifty-two workdays a year off the calendar, I've begun to hear the loving voice of God say, *Son, you can't do it all. Do the part you can; the rest is mine. Leave it to me.*

And if I really do believe that it is God's responsibility to make all things right but still take matters into my own hands, someone might rightly ask about me, "Is he serious? He can't be serious!"

This workshop participant didn't *actually* think I was joking. What he eventually got around to communicating to the program director is that he didn't think I took *him* seriously. During the workshop, I'd suggested that the healthiest and most faithful pattern of work is anchored by a full-day Sabbath taken once every week. It seems he took that as a direct challenge to the importance and gravity of his job, believing that what he was doing was too urgent to "take that many days off."

Now, the man was not wrong, in a sense. The mission of his organization is to care for adolescents. That's not just a high calling; it's a *very* important work. Adolescents are regularly targeted by nefarious agencies and cultural forces, from human traffickers to schemers in the corporate sales world. Meanwhile, the social and emotional patterns developed between the ages of nine to fifteen are some of the most vital and longest lasting in the whole of human development.

It's hard to be a kid.

Which means it's also hard to be someone who cares for kids. I'm a huge fan of the folks who do that work. It takes courage to get into the boat with a populace facing that many storms.

Which makes me think of this story from the Gospel of Mark:

> That day when evening came, he said to his disciples, "Let us go over to the other side." Leaving the crowd behind, they took him along, just as he was, in the boat. There were also other boats with him. A furious squall came up, and the waves broke over the boat, so that it was nearly swamped. Jesus was in the stern, sleeping

on a cushion. The disciples woke him and said to him, "Teacher, don't you care if we drown?"

He got up, rebuked the wind and said to the waves, "Quiet! Be still!" Then the wind died down and it was completely calm.

He said to his disciples, "Why are you so afraid? Do you still have no faith?"

They were terrified and asked each other, "Who is this? Even the wind and the waves obey him!" (4:35–41)

Was that storm real, and did it pose a legitimate threat? Absolutely. But apparently it wasn't as real or pressing as Jesus' need for a nap! I think it's worth noting that Jesus' challenge to his disciples was "Do you *still* have no faith?" In other words, he was saying, "We've been through some stuff, fellas. You've seen me come through for you, and we've weathered worse than this." Which is why the part of this story that really gets me is when, as the disciples were trying to wake up Jesus, one of them said, "Don't you care if we drown?"

I really do understand how taking time away from important work can look like a lack of care. But in the practice of rest, I've learned that the storms and their seriousness shouldn't set the tone for my life. The Love of God for the world should do that. If I live my life at the pace of the urgencies around me, I will almost certainly drown—and it won't be the storm around me that does it; it'll be the unrest and chaos within me.

Consider the following:

- 41 percent of ministers are clinically obese

- 11 percent of pastors report being clinically depressed (consider how many may not feel the freedom to report such a thing)

- 51 percent of pastors have metabolic syndrome (a series of conditions that dramatically heighten the chances they'll have a heart attack, stroke, or type 2 diabetes)

- Ministers share a 6 percent higher heart attack rate than people in other jobs

- 3 in 5 pastors burn out within ten years (that's 60 percent)

- 37 percent of pastors admit to some form of addiction to porn (which often features women who are technically considered adolescents)[1]

It's not the turbulence of adolescent life and culture that is wreaking havoc on the lives of the ministers I coach or care for; it's the turbulence inside their overworked and overstressed souls and psychologies and environments. And if we're serious about doing such a serious job, then we need to be in much better shape while doing it.

My son was born via C-section. Now, I won't go into detail about the procedure outside of saying that surgery is a marvel to me, in large part because, with some exceptions, the mother is awake during the entire thing! That means anesthesia is a key element, and getting that anesthesia right is really, *really* important. So during preparations for her stay in the hospital, my wife filled out a short form on which she noted that her body didn't like certain painkillers. Percocet was among them. She'd taken Percocet after a knee surgery a few years prior and had some terrifying hallucinations. So when she started to speak gibberish on the table *during* the C-section, I asked the anesthesiologist what he was giving her. "Is there any chance you're giving her Percocet?"

> It's not the turbulence of adolescent life and culture that is wreaking havoc on the lives of the ministers I coach or care for; it's the turbulence inside their overworked and overstressed souls and psychologies and environments.

He spun around to face the readout on the machine that was mixing and administering her "cocktail," eyes wide and darting around the screen. His hands immediately ran over the keyboard and buttons while he stuttered, "I'm so sorry. . . . I'm sorry."

It took a few minutes to level things out in Amy's bloodstream. In the meantime, another anesthesiologist walked through the door. He walked straight to our first anesthesiologist and hugged him, hard. In tears, the first anesthesiologist turned to me and said, "He's got you now. You're in very good hands."

Amy ended up just fine, and we got a newborn boy after the whole ordeal. But (and you know this), it could have been far worse. The anesthesiologist knew that too. He cared about the work he was doing enough to know that he was no longer capable of doing the job well.

I get that sometimes you and I get worn out or tired. I get that sometimes we even get exhausted and notice our work is starting to suffer. Those moments can be clarifying and even transformative. But as a patterned way of living, they're downright devastating.

I coach a good number of ministers carrying loads of guilt after years of doing what they now consider damaging to the people and institutions they loved. When exhaustion set in, they just kept plodding along because the work seemed too urgent. They hadn't been healthy, but they often felt like it was better to show up at 60 percent or 50 percent or even 30 percent than not show up at all.

But think about that anesthesiologist.

Was he on the clock? Yes. In fact, there was a patient on the table. But because he cared about the job (and, ostensibly, the patient), he knew he *had* to step away. He wasn't in a condition to do the job with care and wisdom. If I want to care for people as beset with trials as adolescents are, then I *need* to be a healthy human. If my plan to help kids navigate a world seemingly hell-bent on dehumanizing them includes sacrificing my own humanity, I hope someone would pull me aside and lovingly ask, "Are you serious? You can't be serious."

In the quarter century I've worked as a pastor, artist, author, and coach, I've had the great privilege of working alongside women and men doing some of the most vital work imaginable, from providing clean water for people living without it to rescuing children from slavery to providing resources and lifelines to people battling depression. I can't imagine a world without the work they do. I also can't imagine any of that work getting done well and wisely if they aren't the people they are. More to the point, the evils they work to undo are all ways human beings are used, misused, and degraded. I don't think God is interested in trading one system of utility for another. I also don't think God is looking to *use* people to achieve even lofty and beautiful goals. God's way is different, entirely.

In Isaiah 55, God said,

> *"For my thoughts are not your thoughts,*
>
> *neither are your ways my ways,"*
>
> *declares the* LORD.
>
> *"As the heavens are higher than the earth,*
>
> *so are my ways higher than your ways*
>
> *and my thoughts than your thoughts.*

As the rain and the snow

    come down from heaven,

and do not return to it

    without watering the earth

and making it bud and flourish,

    so that it yields seed for the sower and
        bread for the eater,

so is my word that goes out from my mouth:

    It will not return to me empty,

but will accomplish what I desire

    and achieve the purpose for which I
        sent it.

You will go out in joy

    and be led forth in peace;

the mountains and hills

    will burst into song before you,

and all the trees of the field

> *will clap their hands.*
>
> *Instead of the thornbush will grow the juniper,*
>
> *and instead of briers the myrtle will grow.*
>
> *This will be for the LORD's renown,*
>
> *for an everlasting sign,*
>
> *that will endure forever." (vv. 8–13)*

Regardless of how important your work is, it matters as much to God that you "go out in joy" and are "led forth in peace." It matters to God that you are healthy and whole (and even happy) while doing the work he has called you to. Your legacy is not more important to God than the richness of your life while you build that legacy. In fact, it is the Love of God in you that you pass on to people. *That* is your legacy. Which is to say that, for God, there isn't a competition between your work and your well-being.

> It matters to God that you are healthy and whole (and even happy) while doing the work he has called you to. Your legacy is not more important to God than the richness of your life while you build that legacy.

About a year after that confrontation with a retreatant, another young man at yet another Sabbath Keeping workshop voiced a similar concern about the urgency of his work with kids. This time, he offered his question midsession, which meant we could talk. The conversation went something like this:

Him. I just can't see how I can take that much time off and still be effective.

Me. You mean because there's too much to do and all of it is important?

Him. Yeah.

Me. Is it of vital importance that adolescents come to a saving knowledge of the Love of God?

Him. Yes.

Me. And is that the mission of this organization?

Him. Yes.

Me. And is that also your mission?

Him. Yes.

Me: Is that mission worth your soul?

Him. (smiling and giggling a bit now) No . . . I mean, I think I'm supposed to say no.

Me. But you shouldn't have to make that choice, should you? Because doing the work well shouldn't be antithetical to being healthy.

Him. (after a long pause) Yes . . . I think I get it. I'm not being used. I'm being Loved, and I have to know that and live that way so that I can pass that on.

Amen and amen.

Once the room had emptied, I grabbed my notebook and jotted down this short prayer I've been hanging on to ever since:

May I never sacrifice

my health and wholeness

on the altar of productivity;

let my work be rooted

in my full humanity and in grace.

And a small part of me wanted to send it in an email to the gentleman I'd met the previous year. But I didn't. He doesn't need me. God's got him.

Also (and of note), God's got you too.

Questions for Reflection

- Have you ever been too tired to do an important thing well?
- How does it sound to take fifty-two days a year off your work calendar?
- If that scares you a bit, what scares you about it?

Chapter 13

REROUTING THE RACE

or

SABBATH AS AN ACT
OF RESISTANCE

The Sabbath appears as the fourth of the Ten Commandments, introduced in Exodus 20. I think that's notable for two reasons. First, it shows up before the commandments against murder and theft. Think about that for a moment. Before God said, "Don't kill one another" or "Don't steal one another's stuff," he said, "Take a day off every week." Which makes me wonder if, were we to take a day off each week, maybe we wouldn't be killing one another and taking one another's stuff so often. That's about 20 percent joke and 80 percent seriousness. Second, the Sabbath commandment is the first commandment to prescribe an active behavior. The first three commandments are predominantly about the holiness of God and a few things *not* to do because of who God is:

"You shall have no other gods before me.

"You shall not make for yourself an image in the form of anything in heaven above or on the earth beneath or in the waters below. You shall not bow down to them or worship them; for I, the LORD your God, am a jealous God, punishing the children for the sin of the parents to the third and fourth generation of those who hate me, but showing love to a thousand generations of those who love me and keep my commandments.

"You shall not misuse the name of the LORD your God, for the LORD will not hold anyone guiltless who misuses his name." (vv. 3–7)

Then, starting in verse 8 . . .

Remember the Sabbath day by keeping it holy. Six days you shall labor and do all your work, but the seventh day is a sabbath to the LORD your God. On it you shall not do any work, neither you, nor your son or daughter, nor your male or female servant, nor your animals, nor any foreigner residing in your towns. For in six days the LORD made the heavens and the earth, the sea, and all that is in them, but he rested on the seventh day. Therefore the LORD blessed the Sabbath day and made it holy.

"Wait," you might say, "isn't the commandment about *not* working? Doesn't it make it just like the first three?" That's not how I read it. The fourth commandment begins with the word "Remember." Rest isn't just the absence of work. Sabbath rest is the active reconnection of the human soul to its own humanity and to the Source of that humanity. The first thing people are asked to *do* in light of the holiness of God is to rest, specifically by remembering, practicing, and keeping the Sabbath.

I know there is a nearly endless list of theological and textual resources about why the commandments are ordered this way. For my part, I come away recognizing this invitation and commandment is not just important but a key way to connect with God on God's terms rather than my own.

Of course, rest appears in the Scriptures long before its place as the fourth commandment. Before it was commanded as the practice of Sabbath, rest was woven into the fabric of reality. Here it is in the second chapter of Genesis, during the creation poems:

> Thus the heavens and the earth were completed in all their vast array.

> By the seventh day God had finished the work he had been doing; so on the seventh day he rested from all his work. Then God blessed the seventh day and made it holy, because on it he rested from all the work of creating that he had done. (vv. 1–3)

I come away from reading these verses with a lot of questions about what it means to be "done." During my workshops or sermons, I've often cracked a few jokes about what, in the process of creation, might have worn God out to the point of being "done." Usually it's some wisecrack about the complexity of the platypus or the chaotic obstinacy of the United States House of Representatives. But the deeper reality I think this imagery gets at is that God *chose* to rest. I don't think God was exhausted by the energy and focus it took to create dogs and cats on the same day without pet drama. Instead, I think part of what makes this moment sacred is that God, in joy and deep satisfaction with the work of creation, *chose* to rest. It is an act of will rather than necessity.

God acts according to who God is. Rest is part of who God is. The commandment to practice rest, then, is also an invitation to become more like the One Who Made Me and live according to who I am instead of what needs to be accomplished.

Millennia later, by the time those commandments were given, God's invitation wasn't *Work hard and take a break when you need one.* His invitation was *Join me in this way of living and let your life be shaped like mine so that you can experience wholeness, holiness, and blessedness the way I designed things to be.*

> I don't think God was exhausted by the energy and focus it took to create dogs and cats on the same day without pet drama. Instead, I think part of what makes this moment sacred is that God, in joy and deep satisfaction with the work of creation, *chose* to rest.

Since the commandment is to "Remember," I take that to mean that the desire for rest is already in us. I think we long for the kind of rest in which we experience our Belovedness. That's the way God made the world to work, including our own souls. Yet, like other basics to healthy living (forgiveness or mercy or compassion), it's not enough just to feel the need for rest. We still have to choose it and practice it. That choice can be very, very hard.

Theologian and author Walter Brueggemann calls Sabbath rest an "act of resistance."[1] I like that a lot. It places Sabbath keeping in the same stream of thought, action, and urgency as the work of Dr. Martin Luther King Jr. and Malcolm X. I think that's an appropriate place for Sabbath keeping.

Dr. King and Malcolm X resisted a dominant narrative ideology that sought to dehumanize people God Loved. They taught others to resist the underpinning of industries and institutions that believed Black bodies were most valuable as instruments in an economy driven by various forms of slave labor. That ideology was (and is) entirely, dangerously, and tragically wrong. So are the industries and institutions that believe the better part of your eighty-five or so years on this planet are best spent propping up their agenda and mission.

In his book *Sabbath as Resistance: Saying No to the Culture of Now*, Brueggemann wrote, "Sabbath is a bodily act of testimony to alternative and resistance to pervading values and the assumptions behind those values."[2]

One of the "pervading values" Dr. King and Malcolm X set themselves against was utility. The thing that made Black lives matter differently (and in fact less) is that from the mid-1500s to the mid-1800s, African women and men were the engine of the new American economy. Black bodies were useful for labor. The assumption *behind* that value, the value that paved the way for the transatlantic slave trade, was that as long as the dominant populace benefited from that economy, the impact it had on human lives was worth it. That's a lie. There isn't a profit margin large enough or an accomplishment marvelous enough to justify the abuse and devaluating of human beings.

Brueggemann published his book in 2014 for the same reasons that, fifty years earlier, Dr. King and Malcolm X had gathered, protested, and resisted. Because, 113 years after the transatlantic slave trade ended, the same values and assumptions were still in play and wreaking havoc on human life. The civil rights movement was an act of resistance. That resistance was an act of love.

The Sabbath was commanded by God in the shadow of a very recent history of Jewish slave labor in Egypt. It, too, was an act of resistance. And that resistance was also an act of love.

In the book of Matthew, Jesus healed a man by sending unclean spirits into a herd of pigs. The villagers then chased Jesus out of town because they didn't like what it cost them for that man to be made well. In the same way, Malcolm X and Dr. King were both assassinated because those who benefited from that corrupt narrative ideology (let's just call it the status quo) didn't like what resistance might mean for their bottom line. Part of what Brueggemann points to in his book is that when you push against the machinery, don't be surprised when it pushes back.

Early in my touring career, I was fortunate enough to be added to the roster of a very active and successful booking agency. Along with the gift of having someone else put in the hours it took to build and manage a touring calendar, there was a prestige that came with being on a booking agency's roster.

When we started working together, I met with the agency's bosses to talk about strategy and expectations. Mainly, we talked about target regions and the hopes we shared to grow my audience so that I would get more show offers and everyone could make more money. That's when I handed over a list of eight dates in the fall I didn't want them to book.

"What are these dates?"

"Those are Oakland Raiders home games. I'm not available on those dates."

Now, that might sound trite. But I wasn't blocking off those dates because I was a fan of the Oakland Raiders at the time. I mean, I was. But the reason I thought it was worth it to pull eight potential paydays off the table was because I wanted to take my mom to those games. Going to Raiders games was what we did as a family instead of vacations to Disneyland or Tahiti. We didn't have money for Disneyland or Tahiti, but we could purchase season tickets. So, eight Sundays each fall, we'd load up the car and head to the parking lot of the Oakland Coliseum in time for the gate to open at 7 a.m. We'd spend the morning eating breakfast with strangers and listening to or (later) watching the East Coast games before heading inside. It was a McRoberts family tradition and a connection point for all three of us. No matter what else was going on, we shared Raiders football.

After we lost my dad, there wasn't a chance I was going to let that tradition go. Initially, that made some emotional sense to the agency. But over time, those Sundays started to become a problem. More and more people were hiring musicians and speakers (of which I was both) for Sunday gatherings and paying big dollars. Yet there I was, saying no eight times before fall booking even started.

Then there was the season it was ten Sundays.

Rerouting the Race

The Raiders had made the playoffs. I don't think I ever told my mom that I turned down a pretty great gig to be home for that playoff game. (Hi, Mom. You're worth it. Keep reading, and don't call me about this, please.) It wasn't an easy conversation with the booking agency. They were understandably disappointed to miss out on the check I'd been offered.

When we got to the parking lot on the day of the game, my mom handed me an old Oakland Raiders windbreaker and said, "This is what your dad used to wear. I just found it while cleaning out his closet." I put on the jacket and threw my hands into the pockets, where I found a playoff ticket from December 22, 1973. It was a divisional playoff game between the Raiders and Pittsburgh Steelers.

Beloved, I was born January 1, 1974. That means my mom was sitting with my dad in the third deck of the Oakland Coliseum watching the Raiders win a playoff game just a week before giving birth to me. That was the last time she'd been to a playoff game. I'm so thankful I made that choice. It was worth everything it cost me to do so.

The booking agency dropped me not too long after that. But before you go feeling like I was an idiot for sacrificing key aspects of my career at the time when there might have been other ways to care for my mom, or even feeling sad for me because my booking agency dropped me, you should know that, at that same game, Metallica drove into the parking lot on a flatbed truck and played an impromptu show for screaming fans like me. It was one of the coolest live music experiences of my life. It felt like a loving pat on the back from God, saying,

This is my son. With him I am well pleased. He did a good thing for his mom. Here, have some Metallica.

In my own small way, I had resisted the urgencies and pressures of the industry I was in and, along with those pressures, the temptations of "growth" I was offered at the time. In doing so, I lost something important to me that made my work harder, to say the least. But I'd do it again today if it meant ensuring my mom knows, even the slightest bit more, that she's Beloved.

Sabbath resistance isn't as much a blanket critique of organizational and institutional growth as it is a call to evaluate what we mean by "growth." It is a call to consider that if what we think of as growth comes at the cost of well-being, that growth is likely cancerous and should be treated as such. Sabbath keeping pushes back against the forces that would undermine an organization at its core.

When you pull fifty-two days of work off your calendar, it is an act of resistance that is, at its heart, an act of love—love for the organization you care for, love for the people working within it, and love for those who benefit from what the organization is doing. When you

159

say, "No, I can't work that day. That day I've set aside for the renewal of my spirit and mind and body," you also say, "I'll be better for you, and you'll be better if I'm healthier." You are not resisting your organization in some youthful act of childish defiance; you're resisting the cancer in that organization that would undo your organization's health if given enough time. You're calling on the organization to recognize the human shape of those it employs so that it can better serve those human beings who might, in turn, better serve the Beloved human beings the organization seeks to enrich through its work.

Sabbath rest is an act of resistance.

That resistance is an act of love.

Questions for Reflection

- Did/does your family have traditions you've needed to protect from other pressures, including work pressures?
- What do you make of the dominant narrative I referenced in the chapter? Do you see it or hear it too? If so, where?
- What do you think about the connection I made here between Sabbath keeping and the civil rights movement?

Chapter 14

LOVING THE RUN
INSTEAD OF THE RACE

or

SMARTPHONES, TWO-YEAR-OLDS, AND SEEING MYSELF IN A BETTER STORY

You may already be familiar with Macrina Wiederkehr's potent prayer from the book *A Grateful Heart*:

> *Oh God*
>
> *help me*
>
> *to believe*
>
> *the truth about myself*
>
> *no matter*
>
> *how beautiful it is!*[1]

That prayer gets to me just about every time I read it. To some degree because that's not how I expect the phrase to go when it starts. I expect it go a bit darker and get negative. I grew up thinking that when folks say, "Let's get real," we are about to have a conversation about what is worst about one another, or at least what is worst about me. Wiederkehr's prayer seems to suggest that what is most real and most true about us is quite beautiful. That takes some getting used to. I'm working on it.

More than fifty years before Wiederkehr penned that quotable prayer, C. S. Lewis wrote somewhat inspiringly about our relationship to beauty as well. More specifically, in his book *The Weight of Glory,* Lewis wrote about our desire to be contextualized by beauty.

> We do not want merely to *see* beauty, though, God knows, even that is bounty enough. We want something else which can hardly be put into words—to be united with the beauty we see, to pass into it, to receive it into ourselves, to bathe in it, to become part of it.[2]

I think we often travel to beautiful places, watch inspiring shows or movies, and read great books not only because we enjoy them externally but because, internally, our hearts desire proximity to beauty and meaning; we want to be neck-deep in it. Maybe more poignantly stated, I think we want to be meaningful. I think we want to be beautiful.

> I think we often travel to beautiful places, watch inspiring shows or movies, and read great books not only because we enjoy them externally but because, internally, our hearts desire proximity to beauty and meaning; we want to be neck-deep in it.

I often joke about my affinity for (most) things Batman. I'm definitely entertained by the comics and films. But (and this is an odd confession, I know) I also really want, in some way, to *be* Batman.

That's not to say I want to go sneaking around alleys, leaping off rooftops, and beating the snot out of bad guys. I don't have the physical prowess for that kind of thing. The thing that makes me want to be Batman is that I want to live in a Story in which I feel strong and purposeful and clever and victorious. Specific to the Bruce Wayne–Batman mythology, I want to feel like I've got something good to do with the anger I feel at a world that steals dads from their kids and rewards the criminality of the systems that do so. But far from simply being about Batman, I think that desire is a kind of spiritual gravity drawing me into God's Story—a Story in which I get to know I am meaningful, purposeful, victorious, and beautiful.

The catch is that I've become so familiar and comfortable with lesser stories that believing I get to be part of something truly special can be really hard. By "lesser stories," I mostly mean the ones that go something like this:

Be a decent kid, don't get in trouble, graduate with good enough grades so you can get into college so you can get a job so you can buy enough stuff to keep your family happy, and then once your body is mostly used up and tired, spend a couple of years on vacation before you die and hope you left enough money for your kids to do a little bit better at that same thing you just did.

Or sometimes the lesser story goes this way:

As much as you'd like to be happy, don't expect that. Find whatever happiness you can on the road to being useful around here. There's just too much to do for you to be thinking about enjoying yourself while you're here.

Loving the Run Instead of the Race

Both of those stories are pretty bad, right? They almost seem designed to steal any sense of meaning or purpose or joy from our blessed gift of life. Which makes me wonder where a story like that comes from and who would make up a thing like that.

Sadly, those stories were so prevalent and common while I grew up that, as awful as they were, I just figured they were what everyone believed and, therefore, they must be true. It was a foolish fantasy and a waste of time to imagine something better for myself. I unfortunately believed those lesser stories described above for a very long time. It has been quite a journey to believe a different Story for myself and those I love.

I suppose that's why Wiederkehr wrote what she did as a prayer; it's a thing I *want* to be true of me, regardless of how far away it seems from my lived and present reality. I want to get there, and I know I've got some work to do. I also know I'll need some serious help because I can't do it on my own. The practice of rest is the primary way I'm regularly learning to wrestle loose of the grip lesser stories have on me, so I can see myself the way God sees me and maybe pass along some of that same vision to people I care about.

> The practice of rest is the primary way I'm regularly learning to wrestle loose of the grip lesser stories have on me, so I can see myself the way God sees me and maybe pass along some of that same vision to people I care about.

166

This reminds me of my daughter, who, by the time she was two years old, had already developed a somewhat remarkable talent for navigating my phone. She didn't know the lock screen passcode (or at least I don't think she did), but once I unlocked the phone for her, she deftly flipped through screens and recognized apps she liked. Trying to be a good dad, I downloaded a few learning games, and, on occasion, she'd play those. But more than anything else, she wanted to look through my photos to find herself.

In fact, when she wanted my phone, she wouldn't say "phone" or "pictures" (and rarely even said "please"). Instead, she'd just point at the phone and say, "See Katelyn?" Then she'd swipe through images until she saw one of herself. At which point she'd stop, look at the picture for a moment or two, smile, and show it to me, saying, "See? Katelyn!"

I noticed, though, that she almost always missed photos she was in with other people, including photos she was in with me. If she wasn't prominently featured on the screen, she didn't see herself at all. In other words, she struggled to see herself in context. Some of those pictures were of some of her favorite people too! Of course, I knew she was in those pictures, so I'd try to catch one with my finger before she swiped it away, saying something like "There you are, Bird! Can you see yourself?"

She didn't like that.

Not. One. Bit.

It didn't matter that it was my phone. It also didn't matter that

I was trying to help! But . . . it was my phone, and I *did* want to help. So eventually I'd engage in one of the greatest struggles of my adult life: taking my phone back from my own child.

Honestly, I thought keeping up with a mortgage, stemming the tide of some neighborhood injustice, or staying in shape after forty would be the toughest part of adulthood. But no. I think getting my phone back from my kids has probably required the most energy, skill, and emotional support. If you haven't attempted this feat, trying to get a phone back from a child can be a bit like wrestling an alligator covered in grease who also has your phone and won't give it back.

The thing is, I didn't want to *take the phone away* from Katelyn. I wanted her to hand control of the device over to me so I could help her see herself in context. I actually wanted what she wanted; I wanted her to see herself. I think my daughter is living in a big, beautiful Story, and, as her dad, I could help her do that if she would just let go, even a little bit. But she was so committed to the control she had over the device she was using and so satisfied with one way of seeing herself, she wasn't easily willing to hand over control.

> Seeing yourself as part of God's beautiful Story requires you to relinquish your control.

Seeing yourself as part of God's beautiful Story requires you to relinquish your control. For my part, that control shows up in some very specific ways and practices. Maybe you'll resonate with a few of them.

- I control my online profiles with the content I create and push for various platforms and spaces.

- I control my work image by picking and choosing which works to produce and release or which jobs and partnerships to enter into.

- I control my in-person social image with the stories I choose to tell (or not tell).

- And on and on . . .

What's bananas is that I do all of this controlling and strategizing because I want to weave together a Story I feel inspired to live in. All the while, the One Who Holds All Things Together is inviting me into a Story that is beautiful beyond my wildest imaginings; I just spend so much time and energy making up my own story that I don't easily allow God to reframe things for me.

> The One Who Holds All Things Together is inviting me into a Story that is beautiful beyond my wildest imaginings; I just spend so much time and energy making up my own story that I don't easily allow God to reframe things for me.

I love the way Jesus reframes Mary of Bethany's story. In Luke's version of this story, Mary was referred to at one point as "A woman in that town who lived a sinful life" (7:37). Yikes. Imagine that being *your* story. That the people around you primarily refer to you as someone with a sordid past or who had done some things they found distasteful. (Actually, maybe you don't have to. Maybe that's how folks around you have contextualized you. If so, I'm so sorry. That's really hard. Also, they're wrong; that's not who you are. And that's why I desperately hope your life finds context in the Love of God rather than any other kind of metric or machinery.)

Jesus was in the house of a man named Simon when Mary walked in with what the writer called "very expensive perfume" (Mark 14:3). She then poured the perfume over Jesus' head and feet, and while she was doing that, she wept and wet Jesus' feet with her tears. It was a striking and poetic scene. Which made it the perfect time to talk about how much everything cost, didn't it? I'm joking, but that's exactly what the men in the room started doing. Specifically, they started pointing out how much money they could get for the perfume Mary walked in with, as if the real value to be found in the moment was the market value of the perfume. The thing is, as valuable as the perfume might have been, its worth was rooted in and dictated by the same system of metrics and evaluations that devalued Mary's life and experiences in the eyes of the men at the table. Which is why she'd come to Jesus. I'd be very willing to bet she didn't need to be told how much the jar of perfume was worth. It was hers, after all, and she probably knew exactly what it cost. Which means she also knew what it cost to pour it out on Jesus instead of selling it.

I've begun to see my work a bit like Mary saw that jar of expensive perfume. The system of metrics around me educated me on the value of my time and talent and, in no uncertain terms, suggested that they are the most valuable thing available to me, that my strengths and abilities give my life a place in the story of the world around me. I can be *useful*, which is the thing of highest value to be. Which is why it can seem like such a scandal for me to pull one full workday every week off the calendar (and fifty-two from the year) to pour out my time and talents onto Jesus.

I can hear the voices around me (as Mary did) saying, "Why this waste?" But instead of calculating the cost of the perfume, people around me say things like "You could be spending that time building your platform!" Or "You could be developing a side project!" Or "You could be taking on another job to shore up your finances!" The world around us is confounded and even frustrated by our choice to make rest a practice—just as the men in that room were confounded and frustrated by Mary's choice to dump out her valuable perfume on Jesus.

Jesus was unfazed by their complaints and, in fact, took things even further by saying, "Truly I tell you, wherever the gospel is preached throughout the world, what she has done will also be told, in memory of her" (v. 9).

Mary traded in something valuable for something of much greater value. Buying and owning expensive things is a way to obtain and control one's place in the systems of value around us. She'd relinquished that control to God and traded it for the clear knowledge of her place in God's Story, where her value cannot be measured or added to or taken away. That's exactly the trade-off I'm suggesting you make by making Sabbath a regular practice, to take your time and energy—the ways you control your own story and establish your worth—and pour them out on Jesus so you can see yourself folded into the beautiful Story of God and be called Beloved therein.

Now, in theory, that's the role of Beloved community, which most of the folks I know try to find at a local church—a place to live life among a tribe of people who patiently and intentionally look at us with the eyes of God, reminding us regularly who we are in essence. A Beloved community provides a context of unconditional love and grace and belonging. Sadly, too many of the cultural and institutional spaces that are ostensibly making that promise are so driven by success (often masked as "mission") that, once again, the closest thing anyone can come to Beloved is *useful* or *helpful*.

> You're a Beloved One of God whose patient and enduring work is to make all things fully new, including you. And any plan or mission that doesn't start with your Belovedness and then return you to it is a lesser story than the one you actually belong to.

Sometimes these sacred spaces—held together at the seams by staff and volunteers who are themselves coming apart at the seams—become places beholden to stories intended to inspire . . . but instead sometimes exhaust. Even beautiful stories like "We will change this city!" or "We will end global slavery!" are problematic because, no, you're not. That might be a beautiful thing to want and a thing you get to play some part of, but that is not who you are. You're a Beloved One of God whose patient and enduring work is to make all things fully new, including you. And any plan or mission that doesn't start with your Belovedness and then return you to it is a lesser story than the one you actually belong to.

Which brings me back to Bird (my daughter, Katelyn) and why it was important to me that she handed my phone back. Not only because I had calls coming in, but because I wanted her to see herself the way I did when I was taking her picture: precious and brilliant and funny and talented, but above all, entirely Beloved. She's my Little One. She's my Bird. And I love her because she's mine. Period.

Now, it's not at all lost on me that one of the tools by which Katelyn will learn to see her value in the market economy is a device a lot like my phone. How many of us have lost hours worrying about our self-worth or our place in the world because of something that happened on the four-inch screen we were staring at? I'm not sure I can sufficiently describe to you how desperately I hope that, in time, she will still hand that device over to me and say, "I don't see myself clearly right now. This thing has me confused. Can you help me?" I'm going to want to look at what she's looking at and say, "There's a lot going on here. I don't know how much of it is real or true. What I do know is that what is most true of you is that you are amazing. You are Beloved through and through, Bird. How about we put down this thing for a while and go for a bike ride or a walk or play a game, just you and me?"

Questions for Reflection

- Do you spend too much time online or on social media platforms? How is that affecting you?
- Have you ever fantasized or daydreamed you were in a different story? What was that story?
- What part do you think you play in God's Story?

Chapter 15

WHY AM I RUNNING AT ALL?

or

IT IS ONLY THE LOVE OF GOD THAT LASTS

My head was a dizzy mess of painful words and memories. I remember staring into the fire and trying, without success, to offer some of my attention to what my friend Jay was saying. But between the bourbon and the noise in my mind (which the bourbon was intended to drown out), I couldn't grasp his words clearly enough for them to make any sense. At some point, I know he said something about possible next steps and hopeful futures. That was very much like him to do; he was always a hopeful and encouraging friend. I don't remember for sure, but I'm pretty sure I just kept responding with, "Yeah, man. Maybe. I don't know."

A lot of the next several months would sound and feel like that: dazed, intoxicated, but able to muster just enough attention to stay slightly engaged. I'd heard people talk about feeling "dead inside." In fact, I remember my mom using those same words while trying to help me understand what was going on behind my father's eyes for the few months before his suicide. In those last days, he rarely made eye contact with her or with me, and when he did, it seemed like his actual attention was elsewhere. "He wasn't there anymore," my mom said.

I now felt that way too. I felt absent from my own life for weeks and then months. I wasn't "there." I drank myself to sleep most nights because, when the night inevitably set in, my mind would start spinning with anger and sadness at all the ways I wished things had gone. I was haunted by the guilt of knowing I'd let people down and even more by the feeling that God had done the same to me. It scared me to relate to my dad that way, to experience despair. I knew that, at some point, I'd face a lot of what he had faced and in some of the same ways. But I also told myself I wouldn't end up like him.

That wouldn't be me.

It couldn't be.

I needed it not to be me.

I had to be different.

Earlier that evening, before I ended up in Jay's backyard, I'd helped facilitate the final gathering of what was called Shelter. Shelter was the church I'd helped plant over a decade and a half earlier and the work I had considered the most important of my life—a work that was, as of that night, over.

I never counted on it being over.

We'd started meeting in 1998, gathering in the back of a juice bar called Frenzies. It was a tiny space that probably should have held only fifteen to twenty people. Somehow we eventually crammed forty-five people in there. And while that's not "Jet Ski in the Honda Civic Hatchback" impressive, it's not too bad!

We didn't own a sound system or podium or anything like that. So I'd stand next to the open broom closet to preach or lead songs as loudly as I could, with a few mops and cleaning supplies in my peripheral vision. The room smelled like bleach and yeast, but on Tuesday nights, when we stuffed it full of people looking for a spiritual home, it buzzed with the energy of newness and hope. I'd been to enough religious gatherings to know there was something more than just energy and excitement there for me; it felt like a place I could offer the best of myself and maybe even my worst. In the coming months and years, I anchored myself there mentally, emotionally, and vocationally. Shelter became home for me too.

We didn't call it Shelter in the beginning. We referred to it as a "networking night" for younger people who were either disconnected or didn't feel resonance with the institutional culture they'd grown up in. It turned out a lot of folks matched those descriptions, and our networking night just kept growing. Eventually, having a real name for our community felt necessary.

Now, I'm pretty bad with names and titles. In fact, you're reading a book by someone who has released an EP called "Untitled" and a book called *Title Pending*. So you can imagine it was a bit of a process to land on something that might stick. That is, until one Tuesday night when one of our leaders shared a story about snorkeling the coast of some tropical island and uttered the phrase, "You've gotta be willing to swim out farther and into deeper water if you want to see the big turtles."

That settled it. We started calling ourselves "The Big Turtle." Can you imagine inviting someone to something called The Big Turtle and then having to explain why it's not at all like Burning Man or Bonnaroo?

Why Am I Running at All?

When the time came to start taking ourselves more seriously (including a move from Tuesday nights to Sundays, when most churches meet), the conversation about a name was back on the table, this time with far more denominational and institutional weight to it. We settled on the name Shelter because of a song we were singing pretty regularly. Written by Bill Batstone, the song opened with the lyrics, "You have been a shelter, Lord, to every generation."[1] Being the artsy, expressive person I was at the time, I had taken it upon myself to change those lyrics (don't tell Mr. Batstone), so that we sang, "We *will be* a shelter, Lord . . ."

Beloved, it is one thing to identify with the work you're doing. In fact, I think it's appropriate to feel personally connected to your work. It is another thing entirely to identify *as* the work. And as much as I know that's true and even knew it then, I didn't realize I'd done exactly that—I'd allowed myself to slip across that sometimes too-thin line between "I love this thing I do" and "I *am* this thing I do."

> Beloved, it is one thing to identify with the work you're doing. In fact, I think it's appropriate to feel personally connected to your work. It is another thing entirely to identify *as* the work.

I attached myself to the emotional highs and lows of Shelter's birth and growth and change and evolution. I didn't just have my finger on the pulse of our culture; I shared that pulse. If Shelter was healthy and doing well, I felt great. But when things were sideways, I was sideways, and I was personally compelled to straighten them out again. That often came with a lot of long, hard (but usually helpful) conversations with people who were internally tangled up or had concerns about Shelter's theology and practice.

For instance, when we were "blacklisted" by a few other local churches because they'd decided we were an "emergent church," I entered into a series of conversations with those pastors, their leaders, and a few of their congregants. As things turned out, we didn't have many actual theological differences. I think they were a little bit thrown off by the low lights and candles we used. All the while, I took their challenges very personally. I took them far too personally. I took a lot of things far too personally.

I used the word *conversations* above somewhat generously because, as is often the case, disagreements in church aren't as much conversations as they are fights. Disagreements and fights in churches are usually what cause a split or breakdown—the inability to have a particular conversation generously, patiently, and without fear or suspicion. When this happens, people who have known one another for years stop treating one another as complex persons in the process of becoming Beloved, choosing instead to pigeonhole one another along ideological lines.

I knew that happened to a lot of churches and church families. But it wouldn't be us.

It couldn't be.

Why Am I Running at All?

I needed it not to be us.

We had to be different.

We weren't.

Having attached myself to its ups and downs, when Shelter unraveled, I was personally undone. I wasn't undone because "my side" took a hit or lost a battle. I was undone because I never imagined that anything could undo Shelter. I'd imagined that "neither death nor life, neither angels nor demons, neither the present nor the future, nor any powers, neither height nor depth, nor anything else in all creation, will be able to separate us from" one another (Romans 8:38–39).

The second verse of the song we named ourselves after talks about how no matter what calamity comes our way—mountains crumbling, earthquakes, roaring seas—we will lift God's name, even as our hearts are pounding and throats are almost too dry to speak.

I thought Shelter would make it through anything. More than that, I thought "making it through" was part of who we were and part of who I had helped make us. I thought I'd helped build something that would last. I thought that was part of who I was.

That would be us.

It had to be.

I needed that to be us.

We had to be different.

We weren't.

And because what we had made would end, like everything else, I felt very, very lost and needed saving.

Which is pretty much what I told my spiritual director several weeks later. He didn't try to help me fix anything but listened and then asked me a question. Actually, he asked me *the* question.

"Where is God in all this?"

And then he suggested a practice that might help me suss that out. In time, the practice did exactly that. But before I had the time to look back through my life to see God at work in the stories I just shared with you, God met me in Kolkata, India.

I was there with friends who worked with Compassion International, and the hotel we stayed in had hired an artist to build sand art throughout the building. I didn't know the pieces were made of sand until I planted my foot in one of them and smudged it like a clumsy toddler. The artist, who was just a few feet down the hall and working on another mandala, smiled while he stood up and made his way toward me. I stepped away from the mess I'd made of his work saying, "I'm so sorry."

Why Am I Running at All?

"They do not last. It is why I make them."

As he pushed the smudged sand into a pile with the side of his palm, he told me that a much larger mandala had recently been defaced by a vandal not too far from where we were. That mandala was nearly thirty feet across and had taken the artist weeks to build. It took the vandal only a few seconds to ruin almost all of it. Then, just as the artist on the hotel floor in front of me was doing, that mandala artist simply got back on his knees and started placing grains of colored sand, pinch by pinch and grain by grain, back into place.

Just as the vandal's decision to ruin that mandala says something about the person who ruined it, so the making, maintaining, and (sometimes) rebuilding of a mandala says something about its artist. In some religious traditions, that act and art is an homage to impermanence itself, a humble declaration that nothing lasts. Personally, I'm not motivated by that idea.

On the other side of dying with (and dying to) a work I thought would define my life, I've come to more fully give myself over to the "hidden wholeness" Thomas Merton and Parker Palmer wrote about—that which is behind and beneath and above and before both work and rest.

But maybe I am freed by it.

Shelter had been the most significant work of my life, and watching it die while feeling powerless to keep it alive felt like a personal death. So maybe it was. And maybe it needed to be,

at least for me. Because in my religious tradition, there is Life
on the other side of death that isn't available elsewhere. And
on the other side of dying with (and dying to) a work I thought
would define my life, I've come to more fully give myself over
to the "hidden wholeness" Thomas Merton and Parker Palmer
wrote about—that which is behind and beneath and above and
before both work and rest.[2] It is what the ancient Chinese call
the Tao, and it is the thing I've been referring to throughout
this book as, quite simply, the Love of God.

Do I get to make anything permanent? No, I don't. Like the
mandala artist's sand sculptures in Kolkata or any business
venture of my father's, Shelter came to an end because everything ends. I was also beginning to see that making things that
last was not the point.

Because I was a terrible office-hand for my Dad

and I drank too much coffee in college

and I got fired from a day care

and I'd stayed up all night in Mexicali

and I lived on rice and inspiration

and I'd been crooked in Germany

and I got hit in the face with a fistful of quarters

and I got dropped by my booking agency

and I was chased down by a book about rest the same
way I was chased down by the relentless and ever-
patient Spirit of God.

In and through work and rest for many years and through
many seasons, God had been faithfully establishing something
immovable and lasting in me: Belovedness. I hadn't beaten the
things that beat my father down, which was my original hope
and plan. I, too, was beaten down.

I hadn't won.

I'd been saved.

Because it is God who is a shelter to every generation.

Just as it is God who is a sanctuary from every storm.

Over the months and years since that night Shelter ended and I
sat devastated in my friend's backyard, as I have allowed grief
and anger to take their space in my life, what was unearthed
and has endured is that, in work and in rest, I am being woven
together, held together and remade by wiser, more skillful, and
more caring hands than my own. I don't get to build something
that "lasts" in the way I'd hoped and wanted. What I *can* do
(and so can you) is reach out, touch, be energized, inspired, and
shaped by That Which Is Permanent—the Love of God.

Questions for Reflection

- Do you feel personally connected to your work?
- Have you ever overidentified with a project or a job? How did that go?
- How does the idea of impermanence—the idea that you and I don't get to make things that last—sit with you?

AND A FINAL, BONUS QUESTION:

- What have you learned in this book about the rhythm and tension between work and rest?

Epilogue

A SHORT VISIT WITH
FROG AND TOAD

You've probably had that experience in which, because your mind is already in a pattern of thinking about something, you notice connections to it everywhere. That happened the other night as I was putting the finishing touches on this book.

My daughter, who is five at the time of this writing, had selected a pair of stories for me to read as she fell asleep, and one of them was from Arnold Lobel's classic children's book *Frog and Toad Together*. From that book, she chose to read the story titled "The Garden."[1] The story goes like this: Toad notices Frog's beautiful garden and asks how he, too, can have one. Frog, in all his generosity, hands Toad some seeds and tells him that, once he plants them, he'll have a garden "quite soon."

Toad immediately runs home to plant those seeds and, just as immediately, he starts yelling at those seeds to sprout and grow.

Predictably, they don't.

Frog comes running in response to Toad's yelling and tells him he has to leave the seeds alone or he'll frighten them.

But Toad is so anxious to see growth and newness that he just can't leave well enough alone. So, contrary to the advice of his friend Frog, Toad puts in copious amounts of time doing the opposite, choosing instead to work very hard in a number of ways to get those seeds to grow.

He reads to them by candlelight.

They do not grow.

He sings to them.

They do not grow.

He reads them poetry.

They do not grow.

No matter what he does or how he performs, Toad simply cannot manage to get those seeds to grow. He does, though, manage to wear himself out entirely. So he falls asleep.

When he is awoken by his friend Frog, he looks to the ground and finds that, as promised, those seeds have sprouted and begun to break through the ground.

"At last," shouted Toad, "my seeds have stopped being afraid to grow!"

"And now you will have a nice garden too," said Frog.

"Yes," said Toad, "but you were right, Frog. It was very hard work."[2]

That's pretty much how I started my particular journey toward Belovedness. I was committed to growth and newness, and I spent most of my energy performing in every way I could in order to make good things happen. And while that desire in me to work well and effectively was a good one, I had desperately misread the invitation.

You and I were "handed these seeds" and invited into a process that would provide a loving home for our whole lives, including our strengths and talents. We weren't invited to share in it because, like good instruments for the machine, our strengths and talents are necessary for growth and newness. We have been invited in Love so that we can freely and joyfully share in all that goodness. Having misunderstood that invitation, I'd worn myself out and fallen asleep. Thankfully I, too, was awakened by the voice of a Friend.

Wake up and see what is already growing. That's how I've made this all to work, and I want you to join me in it. No, I don't want you to stop singing or reading or playing or writing. I want you working while knowing your work is a way to share this life with me. I also want you to know that when you don't work (either because you can't or because you happily choose not to), you share this life with me. May the growth and newness in your own soul as well as the growth and newness in the soil you work be an expression and outpouring of who you are in and with me: you are Beloved.

Epilogue

May it be so that this book and the stories that make it up can serve as a way for you to hear the voice of God telling you the most fundamental truth about your Story and mine:

You're mine. I love you. I'm proud of you.

ACKNOWLEDGMENTS

My team at W Publishing, Lisa Jackson with Alive Agency.

Amy, Asa, and Katelyn, Mo, and Mom.

The HLC, The Ridgeview Crew, Donna Hatasaki and The Good Way, Compassion International, Frank Tate, Dan Portnoy and Portnoy Media Group.

The Shelter Vineyard Community, Young Life, Heartland Community Church.

Rooted Coffee (where I finished writing most of this).

NOTES

Chapter 1: Getting Off on the Right Foot *or* It All Comes Down to Being Loved
1. Thomas Merton, *No Man Is an Island* (Boulder, CO: Shambhala, 2005), 73.
2. Parker Palmer, *The Active Life: A Spirituality of Work, Creativity, and Caring* (Hoboken, NJ: Jossey-Bass, 1999), 15.
3. Mark Buchanan, *The Rest of God: Restoring Your Soul by Restoring Sabbath* (Nashville: Thomas Nelson, 2007).

Chapter 4: Finding My Stride *or* Falling in Love (with Work) in Mexico
1. Palmer, *The Active Life*, 17.

Chapter 5: Pacing Myself *or* Coffee, College, and Knowing My Limits
1. Motorola, "Droid 2: Digits" (television advertisement), McGarry Bowen, 2010.

Chapter 6: Running with Others *or* Ninety Pounds of Rice and Making Lasting Friendships
1. "You Got Lucky," by Tom Petty and Mike Campbell, recorded by Tom Petty and the Heartbreakers, *Long After Dark*, Backstreet Records, 1982.

Chapter 8: Taking a Breather *or* Exhaustion Isn't Professional
1. Buchanan, *The Rest of God*.
2. Steven Pressfield, *The War of Art: Break Through the Blocks*

    and Win Your Inner Creative Battles (New York: Warner Books, 2002), 75–76.

3. Palmer, *The Active Life*, 44.
4. Jean-Louis Briaud, "Civil Engineers Create Wonders of the World," *Civil Engineering*, July 1, 2021, https://www.asce.org /publications-and-news/civil-engineering-source/civil-engineering -magazine/issues/magazine-issue/article/2021/07/civil-engineers -create-wonders-of-the-world.
5. Christopher Klein, "Construction of the Brooklyn Bridge Took 14 Years—And Multiple Lives," *History*, updated May 21, 2020, https://www.history.com/news/brooklyn-bridge-construction -deaths.
6. "The Story of Hoover Dam—Essays," *Bureau of Reclamation*, updated March 12, 2015, https://www.usbr.gov/lc/hooverdam /history/essays/fatal.html.
7. Klein, "Why the Construction of the Panama Canal Was So Difficult—and Deadly," *History*, October 25, 2021, https:// www.history.com/news/panama-canal-construction- dangers.

Chapter 9: Running Hurt *or* Crooked in Germany and the Gift of Rest

1. Seth Godin, *The Icarus Deception: How High Will You Fly?* (New York: Portfolio, 2012).

Chapter 10: Quitting the Race "For Good" *or* Disconnect and Repair

1. Julia Cameron, *The Artist's Way Every Day: A Year of Creative Living* (New York: Penguin, 2009), 4.
2. Henri J. M. Nouwen, *The Wounded Healer: Ministry in Contemporary Society* (New York: Doubleday, 1972), 63.
3. Buchanan, *The Rest of God*, 129.
4. "Summary Report: 2014 Statewide Survey of United Methodist Clergy in North Carolina," Duke Clergy Health Initiative, https:// divinity.duke.edu/sites/divinity.duke.edu/files/documents/chi /2014%20Summary%20Report%20-%20CHI%20Statewide%20 Survey%20of%20United%20Methodist%20Clergy%20in%20 North%20Carolina%20-%20web.pdf.
5. Helen H. Lemmel, "Turn Your Eyes Upon Jesus," published in Glad Songs by British National Sunday School Union, 1922.
6. Lemmel, "Turn Your Eyes Upon Jesus."

Chapter 12: I'm Not Running to "Win" or Trading Your Soul for the World
 1. "Summary Report," Duke Clergy Health Initiative.

Chapter 13: Rerouting the Race or Sabbath as an Act of Resistance
 1. Walter Brueggemann, *Sabbath as Resistance: Saying No to the Culture of Now* (Louisville, KY: Presbyterian Publishing, 2014), 31.
 2. Brueggemann, *Sabbath as Resistance*, 21.

Chapter 14: Loving the Run Instead of the Race or Smartphones, Two-Year-Olds, and Seeing Myself in a Better Story
 1. M. J. Ryan, ed. *A Grateful Heart: Daily Blessings for the Evening Meals from Buddha to the Beatles* (York Beach, ME: Conari Press, 1994), 152.
 2. C. S. Lewis, *The Weight of Glory and Other Addresses* (New York: HarperOne, 2009), 42; emphasis in original.

Chapter 15: Why Am I Running at All? or It Is Only the Love of God That Lasts
 1. "To Every Generation," Bill Batstone (San Clemente, CA: Maranatha! Music, 1986).
 2. Parker Palmer, *A Hidden Wholeness: The Journey Toward an Undivided Life* (San Francisco: Wiley, 2004), 4.

Epilogue
 1. Arnold Lobel, "The Garden," *Frog and Toad Together* (New York: HarperTrophy, 1979), 18–29.
 2. Lobel, 29.

ABOUT THE AUTHOR

Justin McRoberts lives in Martinez, California, with his wife and their kids, Asa and Katelyn. Along with writing books like this one, Justin coaches artists, ministers, and entrepreneurs. He also travels regularly to lead retreats, teach, and perform. Justin really likes peanut butter (both chunky and smooth) and loves wrestling with his two kiddos. He lets them win.

IT IS WHAT YOU MAKE OF IT

Creating Something Great
from What You've Been Given

JUSTIN McROBERTS

With warmth, wisdom, and humor, McRoberts shares key moments from his twenty-plus years as an artist, church planter, pastor, singer-songwriter, author, neighbor, and father, passing on lessons and practices learned about making something good from what we've been given rather than simply accepting things as they are.

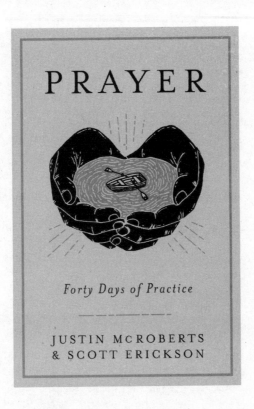

PRAYER

Forty Days of Practice

JUSTIN MCROBERTS
& SCOTT ERICKSON

We pray because we are human, not because we are religious. Something in our nature points beyond itself, and something in us searches for and desires personal connection with God. Prayer is a simple yet profound guide to facilitate the instinctively human desire to pray.